ISBN 978-1-330-02669-4
PIBN 10007295

NEW EVIDENCES IN PSYCHICAL RESEARCH

New Evidences in Psychical Research

A RECORD OF INVESTIGATIONS, WITH SELECTED EXAMPLES OF RECENT S.P.R. RESULTS

BY

J. ARTHUR HILL

WITH AN INTRODUCTION BY

SIR OLIVER LODGE, D.Sc, F.R.S.

Principal of the University of Birmingham

LONDON

WILLIAM RIDER & SON, LTD.

164 ALDERSGATE STREET, E.C.

1911

RICHARD CLAY & SONS, LIMITED,
BREAD STREET HILL, E.C., AND

TO MY FRIENDS

F.K., I.O., AND M.E.N.

"I, at least, will shun the weakness of philosophising beyond my depth. . . . What is the use of pretending to assurances we have not, respecting the other life? . . . If there is a wish for immortality, and no evidence, why not say just that? If there are conflicting evidences, why not state them? If there is not ground for a candid thinker to make up his mind, yea or nay—why not suspend the judgment? I weary of these dogmatisers, I tire of these hacks of routine, who deny the dogmas. I neither affirm nor deny. I stand here to try the case. I am here to consider, σκέπτειν, to consider how it is."

(Emerson: *Montaigne; or, The Sceptic.*)

PREFACE

It is desirable, in the interests of psychical research, that experiences of apparently supernormal nature should be put on record, if they reach a fairly high evidential level. The incidents described in the following pages seemed worth chronicling, though no claim is made that any or all of them can be regarded as supplying proof of any particular theory. I thank the friends who have so kindly allowed me to make use of their results.

It appeared, also, that a selection of cases giving an idea of recent S.P.R. investigation might be useful to readers who have no time for the study of very lengthy reports. A few chapters have accordingly been added, dealing with such investigation. I have to thank the Council of the Society for Psychical Research for permission to quote from the *Proceedings*. For all opinions in the text, the responsibility is mine.

J. A. H.

Bradford,
December 1910.

INTRODUCTION

My friend Mr. J. Arthur Hill, having been more or less concerned in various remarkable experiences, thinks it desirable to publish them, and at the same time to discuss briefly the general subject from a reasonable point of view and in the light of a considerable knowledge of what has been done by others.

He has asked me to introduce his little book to the Public; and accordingly I have pleasure in testifying to the careful and responsible truthfulness which characterises his presentation, and to the unemotional habit of mind with which he regards these phenomena.

Without vouching for the details of events many of which are outside my own knowledge, I nevertheless commend the narrative as well worthy of study, and the discussion of possible explanations as sane and likely to be helpful to many readers. So far as a book dealing with a subject of this obscurity can be trustworthy I consider that this book is of that nature; and the simplicity of its treatment should make it widely read.

Oliver Lodge.

September 1910.

CONTENTS

CONTENTS

NEW EVIDENCES IN PSYCHICAL RESEARCH

A RECORD OF INVESTIGATIONS, WITH SLECTED EXAMPLES OF RECENT S.P.R. RESULTS

CHAPTER I

GENERAL CONSIDERATIONS

ANY one who writes on psychical research without having clear-cut convictions as to the explanation of the phenomena, is in a rather unenviable position. If he fails to ascribe them to fraud or "electricity," he will be regarded by the outsider as a credulous crank, or—to vary the epithet to that by which the Beach-comber designated his friend Mr. Andrew Lang—as a "superstitious muff"; while, on the other hand, if he declines to give in to "spirits" he will be accused, in some quarters, of constitutional unbelief, inability to make logical inferences from the facts, or unconquerable bias and unfairness. He may thus fall between two stools.

But we may perhaps venture to hope that a few righteous men may be found, who will pick him up again. Public opinion is slowly but surely becoming educated: is gradually realizing that it is unwise to come to conclusions in a hurry; that in this very complex world there is no telling what may happen, and that therefore it is unsafe to reject a statement as being necessarily untrue just because, to our prejudiced minds, it seems absurd. It is a question of evidence; let us defer decision until sufficient evidence has been accumulated. Like Plutarch, let us sit on the fence. For "to give entire credit to them [stories of speaking statues, in this case] or altogether to disbelieve them, is equally dangerous, on account of human weakness. . . . It is best to be cautious, and to avoid extremes." It may cheerfully be admitted, that—to quote a contemporary of Plutarch's—"lovers of the marvellous are too prone to heighten the marvels they hear tell of, by adding touches of their own; and thus they debase truth by alloying it with fiction." In which remark of Pausanias, the founder of modern scientific method would have heartily concurred. But, he would continue, "rarities and reports that seem uncredible are not to be suppressed or denied." Accumulate the evidence, and stick close to objective experience; for "men have withdrawn themselves too much from the contemplation of nature, and the observations of experience, and have tumbled up and down in their own reason and conceits," showing a regrettable "impatience of doubt, and haste to assertion without due and mature suspension of judgment. For the two ways of contemplation are not unlike the two ways of action commonly spoken of by the ancients: the one plain and smooth in the beginning, and in the end impassable; the other rough and troublesome in the entrance, but after a while fair and even: so it is in contemplation; if a man will begin with certainties, he shall end in doubts; but if he will be content to begin with doubts, he shall end in certainties." (*Advancement of Learning*, § 8.)

I am not so sure that he *will* end in certainties. He may continue all his life in doubt. But at least he will have the consolation that he has not led any one astray by unjustified assertion. In psychical matters, even more than in others, there has been too much cocksureness on both sides. Mr. James Robertson, speaking of some controls,[1] says, "I am as certain as I am of anything that I have held converse with 'Joseph Priestley,' the discoverer of oxygen, whom religious bigotry forced to flee from Birmingham to America on account of his Unitarian opinions," and he

[1] *Spiritualism: The Open Door to the Unseen Universe*, p. 50.

also claims acquaintance with the spirits of J. S. Mill and Harriet Martineau; while Mr. John Lobb goes one better, and interviews Dickens, Carlyle, and Shakespeare, who—judging by the report—must have deteriorated terribly since "passing over," for they twaddle atrociously.[1] On the other hand, Mr. Frederic Harrison tells us that "to talk to us of mind, feeling, and will continuing their functions in the absence of physical organs and visible organisms, is to use language which, to us at least, is pure nonsense."[2] Professor Münsterberg is even more downright, for he says, referring to trance-mediumship, that "the facts as they are claimed do not exist, and never will exist, and no debate makes the situation better."[3] And no doubt many sensible folks, unacquainted with the subject, will be prepared to class it, without study, along with that witchcraft which, according to Reginald Scot, was "incomprehensible to the wise, learned or faithfull, a probable matter to children, fooles, melancholike persons or

[1] *Talks with the Dead*, pp. 41, 42, 44, 52.

[2] *Philosophy of Common Sense*, p. 217.

[3] *Psychology and Life*, p. 253. Professor Münsterberg is quite Canute-like in giving his orders to Nature as to what shall happen and what shall not. Or, shall we say, ostrich-like, in hiding his head and vowing that there is nothing to see? Certainly he has not yet learnt the lesson which Canute (in the story) taught his courtiers.

papists"; [1] and they will cheerfully affix, in their minds, the second of Scot's four labels to all those misguided individuals who devote any of their time to investigation of these matters.

Such pronouncements as these, on whichever side, seem to me premature, and harmful to science. The attitude of Plutarch and Bacon is preferable to such hasty dogmatism, and is indeed, I think, the ideal attitude to adopt. Some theorizing of course is inevitable, and hypotheses can only be tested by adopting them, provisionally, and seeing how they work—how far they fit the facts. But it is necessary to keep a sharp eye on the hypotheses, lest they stiffen into doctrines; or, rather, to keep a sharp eye on ourselves, lest we become so enamoured of a hypothesis that we try to make new facts fit it, instead of being guided by them to a perhaps truer explanation. In the infancy of a science, theory is of less importance than careful observation. We must make sure of our facts, before beginning to fit them into their places in the mosaic.

So much on the general aspect; now to come a little nearer the particular.

Psychical Research includes a large variety

[1] *Discoverie of Witchcraft* (1584), *Cambridge History of English Literature*, iii., p. 113.

of phenomena. Some are admitted as occurring, but in need of study and explanation—such as the curious symptoms of multiple personality of the "Sally Beauchamp" kind [1]—while others are alleged but disputed, such as the various supernormal phenomena of Spiritualism. No one can yet decide anything about the relative importance of these different phenomena, for all of them—all that the future will certify as actually occurring, that is—will have some kind of bearing on our conception of the nature and destiny of human personality. For the present, however, the position of greatest prominence is given to those happenings which more or less directly suggest that human beings survive the death of their bodies, retaining the memories and loves of earth, and communicating at times with those who are left behind. It is natural enough that anything which suggests this, should immediately and principally engage our attention; for we all have a vital interest in the question of what really happens to us when we die. A few words, however, concerning other phases of the research, are perhaps desirable.

There is a well-marked class of alleged facts, usually known as "the physical phenomena of Spiritualism." These alleged facts include

[1] *The Dissociation of a Personality*, Dr. Morton Prince.

raps, movement of objects without contact or normal means of impulsion, touches by apparently-material hands which are not the hands of the sitters, materialization of spirit forms, *apports*, and the like. Concerning all these, I have to say that I have had little or no experience in this particular direction, and that I have—consequently—little or no belief. Several of my friends have had the luck to get good table-levitations apparently without contact and in a good light, and I cannot entirely ignore their testimony—particularly as one of them, in whose house the sittings were held, is a strong anti-spiritualist as well as an exceptionally keen observer. And, in common with many other readers, I have been considerably impressed by the Report on Eusapia Palladino in which Messrs. Baggally, Carrington, and Feilding—experienced investigators and hitherto hardened unbelievers—have announced their conversion to the belief that, whatever the cause, the things happen. But it is no more than an impression. The conviction of years, that these things *cannot* happen—however unscientific, as I admit—is not shaken by mere reading. Indeed, I doubt if I should believe in some of these things, even if I saw them. Seeing is not always believing.[1] The possi-

[1] Mr. Lang expresses similar distrust of his own senses

bilities of conjuring are so great that it is dangerous for a non-expert to trust his senses in these fields of investigation, particularly if a paid medium is present. And, even if not, there may be some motive for fraud, other than the financial one. Some person present may have a turn for practical joking, or may have some mental abnormality which predisposes him to the production of marvels, just for the sake of mystery-mongering.[1] This may even be done subconsciously, in a state approaching trance; and the performer may not be morally blameworthy, being irresponsible for his actions. And it must be remembered that in these sittings the medium —paid or unpaid, conscious or entranced—has a great advantage over the platform conjurer. The latter has to produce his phenomena at a given time; the former can wait for his opportunity. And, if the conditions are too stringent—the observers too keen—he can always say that the spirits won't come. It is heads I win, tails you lose. If the sitters are deceivable, they are deceived, and the medium wins;

(*Cock Lane and Common Sense*, p. 22), but disclaims *all* convictions, "negative and affirmative." But if he really had attained this admirable state of acrobatic balance, would not actual experience, under test conditions, pull him over on the affirmative side?

[1] Dr. Maxwell records cases in point: *Metapsychical Phenomena*, pp. 78, 92, 128, 381.

if they are not, they lose—both the phenomena and their money. And indeed it is doubtful if fraud-proof conditions can be devised. A medium who makes a living at the trade, and is therefore in constant practice, may be expected to be more than a match for any layman. For myself, I confess that I have little interest in this branch of the subject, for I see no possibility of attaining safe conclusions. If I could not trust my own observation—and, like Professor Münsterberg, I am quite sure that a very moderately clever trickster would outwit me—still less can I trust the observation of others. Therefore, in short, while admitting the impressiveness of the Report just mentioned, I am nevertheless unconvinced. Even if there was no fraud, the explanation may be "collective hallucination."

And, even if these phenomena were established as occurring without normal causation, they would not prove anything except the existence of a force unrecognized by orthodox science. It is absurd to say that they would prove "spirit-origin." In a series of sensational "exposure-articles" which appeared last year in a popular magazine, it is remarked by a person who poses as an expert but who gives himself away in almost every paragraph, that these minor physical phenomena are "all that I myself require to become a convinced spiritualist." And this gentleman apparently considers himself a hard-headed unbeliever! He seems to me, on the contrary, to be extraordinarily credulous, as well as astonishingly illogical. Why should it necessarily be "spirits," if a table *does* waltz about without being touched? There is no logic in such a supposition. It is like the reasoning of a savage who, ignorant of guns, attributes superhuman power to the white man, because this latter can kill at a distance, without seeming to throw anything. In each case, the argument is from ignorance, not from knowledge. "I don't understand how this can be; therefore it is the work of a spirit, or a god, or a devil." Which, of course, does not follow. On this point, Sir Oliver Lodge remarks: "If asked: Do I associate physical movements and other physical phenomena with the continued existence of deceased persons? I must answer I do not." (*Proceedings S.P.R.*, xvii., p. 49.)

Another curious phase, also deeply tinged with fraud, is that of so-called spirit-photography. Here, again, I have little or no belief, though I have no *a priori* negative judgment to make. There are many actinic rays which are invisible to us; and if we imagine an object which reflects some such rays while remaining transparent to ordinary light-rays, there is not much difficulty in conceiving that the camera may photograph something which is really there, though invisible to us. If a spirit can build up a semi-material form—say, out of some such stuff as the ether—the thing is credible enough. It is a question of evidence as to whether the phenomenon happens, or not. Personally, I have come across only one case that impressed me, and it was not convincing. But it was curious. I will describe it shortly.[1]

On May 15, 1905, between 12 and 1 o'clock, Mr. Binns, photographer, of S—— (a small market town in Lincolnshire), took a photograph of a labourer named Warren. The plate used was the first of a new packet of "Ilfords," purchased that very day. The only persons present in the room were the photographer and the sitter. Nothing abnormal was seen or expected. The people concerned are none of them spiritualists.

The plate was developed on the 19th, and showed, in addition to the sitter, the figure of a man, dressed in ordinary clothing, superposed on the portrait of Warren.[2] The face was quite distinct, also the turn-down collar,

[1] An account of this case appeared in the *Occult Review* for March 1910, with several reproductions of the photographs concerned.

[2] Its position and clear focus disprove any supposition of the well-known dodge of a background painted with sulphate of quinine. The form's face is in the sitter's chest.

tie, cuffs, and watch-chain. It was very unspiritual-looking, and of course suggested ordinary double exposure. But the curious thing is that the figure is a perfect likeness of Warren's cousin (a Mr. Ground), who, so far as we can make out, had never been photographed by Binns, and who, at the time of the incident, happened to be lying in a hospital fifteen miles away, suffering from a gunshot wound from the effects of which he died ten days later. The photographer states in the most solemn and emphatic manner that not only had he never photographed Mr. Ground, but that he was unaware of his existence. The form appearing on the plate was therefore quite strange to him.

No photograph of Mr. Ground is known to exist except one in which he appears in militia uniform, aged about eighteen. At the time of his death he was thirty-four, and of course very different in appearance. It seems, therefore, unlikely that any existing photograph had served as a copy.

There is no apparent motive for fraud, for Binns is (or was, for he is now out of the business) an ordinary photographer, and he stood to lose, not gain, by getting any sort of uncanny reputation. He is well known to a friend of mine (the vicar of M——) whose choirmaster is Binns's brother; and this friend vouches for the integrity of all concerned. And it certainly seems difficult to account for the affair by accident. Mr. Ground had not been photographed by Mr. Binns, and, moreover, the packet of plates was a new one.[1] I suppose the spiritistic explanation would be that Ground, finding himself partially free from his body (he seems to have been probably unconscious at the time), became aware of his cousin being photographed, and was able somehow to produce a photographable thought-form of himself. But I do not entirely accept such an interpretation. The incident is curious, and my friend the vicar is quite convinced that some supernormal agency was concerned; but so much depends on the reliability of Binns (of whom I know nothing discreditable, and to whom an apology is due for the apparent suspicion) that it is dangerous to come to any definite conclusion in the matter. The most that can be said, is, that such cases seem worth investigating. Perhaps we may ultimately come across one in which normal agencies can be satisfactorily excluded. Until then, judgment must be suspended.

Stories of such astral travelling—minus the photography—are told in all ages and among

[1] *Accidental* double exposure is disproved by the clearness of the background, which coincides with that of many other photographs taken by Mr. Binns and seen by me.

all peoples; and it is possible that there may be some truth in it. The following is a curious modern case which supports the notion. Mr. Wilmot was crossing from Liverpool to New York. The passage was very stormy. On the night following the eighth day he dreamed that he saw his wife come to the door of his state-room. Here she hesitated, seeming to discover that the room had a second occupant. Finally, she advanced, kissed him, and withdrew. On waking, Mr. Wilmot found his fellow-passenger, whose berth was above but not directly over his own, leaning on his elbow and regarding him fixedly. "You're a pretty fellow," said the room-mate at length, "to have a lady come and visit you in this way." Asked for explanations, he described what he had seen, while lying wide awake. It tallied exactly with Mr. Wilmot's dream. When the latter reached home, his wife told him that she had been anxious about him, and had "visited" him one night, finding him in a state-room with another occupant in an upper berth, who was awake and who stared at her. The time and the details corresponded with the experience of Mr. Wilmot and his room-mate.[1]

In the following chapter will be found a similar though less detailed experience, in which the "traveller" is a friend of my own.

[1] Myers's *Human Personality*, i., p. 682; *Proceedings S.P.R.*, vii., p. 41.

CHAPTER II

THE TELEPATHIC AND OTHER PHENOMENA OF MRS. NAPIER

THE present chapter will describe a few experiences of a friend of mine who possesses what for want of a better name we call "psychic faculties," but who is in no sense of the word a "professional."

Mrs. Napier—as I will call her—is a lady in early middle age, living a rather quiet country life, though active in charitable works. She belongs to a family of means and position, as did also her husband, whose widely-lamented death occurred not long ago. She is domesticated but sociable, a good musician and landscape painter (as a hobby), very fond of animals, flowers, and outdoor life. She is of exceptional physical strength, and, until recently—when she was thrown from a carriage and sustained slight injuries which have compelled avoidance of violent exercise—she enjoyed enviably perfect health. I mention this because it is fashionable in some quarters to regard "psychic" folks as invariably weak and neurotic. Even Mr. Lang—

probably as a sop to the Philistines, for he surely knows better—remarks that in British Guiana, "as elsewhere, hysterical and epileptic people make the best mediums."[1] However it may be in British Guiana, it certainly is not so nearer home. Our hypnotic specialists come across much hysteria and epilepsy, but they seem to find little or no mediumistic power; so little, that Dr. Bramwell does not believe even in telepathy. And, as to the sensitives with whom the S.P.R. has had its recent results, I am not aware that they show any morbid symptoms. One of them, at the time of Mr. Piddington's report, could spend a day fox-hunting, which, as Mr. Piddington suggests, does not point to much degeneracy.[2]

Mrs. Napier is not a spiritualist, has never attended a spiritualistic *séance* or meeting, has never even seen any trance-speaker, automatic writer, or other medium, and, until after the experiences which I shall describe, had read nothing of the literature of the subject, except a few odd copies of *Light*. In religion she is a good Churchwoman, and her social surroundings are of very orthodox Anglican type.

The form which her experiences most usually take, is that of vision in a kind of trance, or, sometimes, what has been called

[1] *Cock Lane and Common Sense*, p. 39.
[2] *Proceedings S.P.R.*, vol. xviii., pp. 303–4.

"travelling clairvoyance." The condition generally comes on when she is in bed, but is very different from sleep. It is always preceded by a tingling feeling, running through the body from head to foot, and very similar to that produced by a galvanic battery. Cataleptic rigidity follows, and apparitions begin to be seen, usually of unknown people; or, as sometimes, there is a painful feeling of "getting out of the body," and then a sensation of rushing through space—a sensation "delightful beyond description"—to some distant town, whence veridical information, of a kind which guessing, inference, or previous knowledge would not account for, is brought back.[1] In one of these journeys, for example, she saw a friend getting into a train at a certain station in a town a hundred miles away. She had no normal knowledge of this friend's whereabouts on that day; but it turned out that the vision was true. This might, however, be due to chance. The following is a better example.

[1] Jerome Cardan had, in addition to a Socratic "clairaudience," a similar faculty "of passing out of his senses as into ecstasy whenever he will, feeling when he goes into this state a sort of separation near the heart as if his soul were departing, this state beginning from his brain and passing down his spine, and he then feeling only that he is out of himself."—Tylor, *Primitive Culture*. Ref. is to Cardan's *De Varietate Rerum*, 1556, cap. xliii.

In a recent experience of this kind, Mrs. Napier, after the usual feeling of "travelling," seemed to find herself in her old home, sixty miles away from where she lives. She had tried to "go," for she had a feeling that her father, who is an invalid, was worse. Arrived "in spirit" at the house, she went up-stairs, and into her father's room. As soon as she got within the door, she saw her father sitting up in bed, and evidently worse; he turned his head, saw her, and cried out "*Why, there's Mabel!*" She was at this point overcome by the faintness and the "drawn-back" feeling which precede the end of each of these experiences, and, after the rushing return through space, woke up in her body once more. She immediately wrote home, describing the incident. Next morning, however, there came a letter from her step-mother (*i. e.* the letters had crossed in the post) saying that the invalid had been worse, and during the period of attack had seemed to see his daughter standing by the door. He had then called out her name, saying "*There's Mabel!*" or some such phrase. The times coincided closely, so far as can be ascertained. It is noteworthy, however, as indicating the mental nature of these experiences, that the percipient described his daughter as wearing a pink gown; while as a matter of fact she was wearing at the moment a blue dress—which, by the way, he had never seen. The incident occurred at about 10 a.m., and Mrs. Napier was lying down in her room.

I do not press this as a particularly good example of an evidential case. Chance coincidence cannot be quite excluded. And this is the more to be considered, as on one or two occasions a vision has presented details which were *not* true. This incident, therefore, is presented as an illustration rather than as evidence. But I believe that of some at least of these experiences, chance coincidence is not the correct explanation. The following case, though still not amounting to unquestionable proof, is strongly suggestive of some supernormal exercise of faculty. I give it in Mrs. Napier's own words, written out and sent to me a few weeks after the event. (Such incidents ought to be recorded, and the record sent to some responsible person, *at once*, in order that there shall be no time for lapse of memory on points of detail. Mrs. Napier has kindly promised to inform me of any future experience of this kind, immediately on its occurrence.)

"An old friend of ours came to spend the week-end with us, a few weeks ago. He departed, as was his custom, by the nine o'clock train on Monday morning.

Soon after his departure, I went up-stairs, and, a feeling of drowsiness coming over me, I lay down for a few minutes. No sooner had my head touched the pillow than I distinctly felt the vibration, and heard the noise, of a train in swift motion; and then it seemed to me that this friend I speak of was beside me, talking to me, and telling me to be careful of some valuable papers which he had left in a drawer of the writing-table, and which he had forgotten to take with him. Then he was silent, but I could still see him, and could hear and feel the vibration of the train. Then, all in a moment, I felt jerked off the seat, and felt a sharp pain in my back as though it were broken; then the next second I was back in my room again, though I still seemed to feel the pressure of his hands on my shoulders.

"As it afterwards turned out, the gentleman *had* left these papers—quite unknown to me, of course—and at the time of my vision he was wishing I might find and care for them, which I did. A curious additional circumstance is that his train, on reaching his destination, stopped with a jerk which threw him on his back, causing severe pain."

This looks like a mixture of telepathy and clairvoyance. For a similar but more elaborate case (Mrs. Storie's) cf. *Phantasms of the Living*, i., p. 370, quoted in *Human Personality*, i., p. 144.

Mrs. Napier also finds that she is often warned of visitors before they arrive; but in these cases it is difficult to exclude chance. A recent case, however, was rather good. Mrs. Napier was at the piano one Sunday, after lunch. Suddenly, half-way through a piece of music, she stopped and said, "Major Hall is coming; he has just started from home." Her sister ridiculed the idea, for their friend

Major Hall, who lives four miles away, makes it a rule to stay about home on Sunday afternoons, and had never called on them on that day. Mrs. Napier, however, stuck to her point, adding that the Trents were coming also, and Mr. Trowbridge. And they all duly turned up, and stayed to tea and dinner!

I pass now to a striking case of another kind; and, to make the narrative easier to follow, I again give Mrs. Napier's own words, as nearly as possible. She sent me an account of the incident, in a letter, soon after its occurrence in August 1906.

I had gone to bed very tired, after a dinner-party, and—if truth must be told—not in the best of tempers. Just as I was going off to sleep, I began to feel the electrical tingling which always precedes visions. I fought against it for all I was worth, but had to give in, though making up my mind that I would neither see nor hear, if I could help it However, as it soon turned out, I could not prevent it for beside me I heard an agonized voice say :—

"Mabel, Mabel, for God's sake pray for me!"

I am ashamed to record my reply, and can only plead my tiredness in extenuation. I said :—

"Pray for yourself, as I do! I ask nobody to pray for *me!*"

Then it seemed to me that somebody knelt down beside my bed, and a head was bowed upon the clothes. I looked, and saw a head which seemed rather familiar, though the voice had awakened no memories. So I said :—

"Lift up your face, so that I may see you. You address me by my name—what is yours?"

The form at once lifted its head up, and I recognized him as a friend of my girlhood's days—Anthony Grace by name. Softened by the pain in his face, I immediately changed my tone.

"Anthony, let me help you!" I said. "I will, with all my heart: only show me the way."

"Pray for me, pray for me!" came the answer. "I'm dead; can't you see I'm dead?"

"No," I replied, "you do not look dead." Nor did he. I promised to do what he wished, and his face lost some of its pain as he thanked me. He remarked about the trouble he had had to find me, and promised—in response to my request—to try to reach me again. But I have seen nothing of him since.

[Notes from later letters, referring to the above.]

At the time of this occurrence (August 1906) we knew nothing of Anthony Grace's health or general circumstances. He belonged to a part of the country which I had left long before. I had seen him for about ten minutes at a railway station early in 1905, but with this exception I had not seen him for ten years. He passed out of my life before I was twenty-one, and at the time of my vision we knew nothing about his condition, and had no reason to expect his death or any illness.

But it turned out afterwards, when my sister—whom I had immediately told of my experience—visited that part of the country, and made inquiries, that *he had died in August* 1906. Unfortunately, I forgot to note the exact date of my vision, so we cannot find out how nearly it coincides with Grace's death. Probably some hours elapsed between the two, for he died suddenly, while dressing in the morning (unexpectedly and without previous serious illness) and my vision would occur about midnight. But my sister and I are sure that we had no normal knowledge of his death. If we had heard of it, we should certainly have remembered.

On another occasion, Mrs. Napier was alarmed by the apparition of a man, who carried a gun under his arm and a brace of pigeons in one hand. He was quite natural and lifelike, and she would have mistaken him for a living man if she had not remembered that she had carefully locked her door. He advanced into the room, and threw down the pigeons on the bed. Mrs. Napier immediately experienced a peculiarly violent feeling of repulsion which she could not understand; she is quite accustomed to these curious visitations, and they are generally not repellent or objectionable. Then the man spoke—

"You don't know me?"

(*Mrs. N.*) "No."

"Your father knew me well enough. I died over twenty years ago. I'm Tom Wyndham. I used to call your father 'Bob.'"

And he vanished. Mrs. Napier did not remember hearing the name before, but on her next visit home she asked her father if the name was known to him. He asked why she wanted to know, and she gave some kind of evasive reply, for her people disapprove of "this kind of thing." He went on to say, however, that Tom Wyndham had been a friend of his in youth, that he died over twenty years ago, and that, though good-hearted, he had been a wild sort.

"In what way?" asked Mrs. Napier.

"Well," replied her father, "he cared for nothing but sport of a low kind, chiefly pigeon-shooting; and at the end he died raving mad through drink."

Mrs. Napier now understood her feeling of repulsion. But there was one other point.

"What did he call you, father?" she asked.

"He called me 'Bob,'" he replied. "He was the only one of my friends who did so. As you know, I have always had a strong objection to the abbreviation."

I do not propose to discuss the various explanatory hypotheses which these experiences suggest. In the first place, we cannot guarantee the absolute accuracy of the report; for we have to depend, to some extent, on Mrs. Napier's memory. This, however, happens to be a very good one, and it is also to be noted that the accounts were written out, and in my possession, soon after the events occurred: further, I have the corroborative testimony of Mrs. Napier's sister, with regard to the incidents in which she was concerned. I have not much doubt about the essential accuracy of the report, and I feel that some apology is almost due to Mrs. Napier and her sister for considering it even debatable. However, they understand the necessity of considering all the points, and will be indulgent accordingly.

As an illustration of psychic faculty in a non-spiritistic setting, I will give as a close to this chapter a curious case of apparent premonition as distinguished from precognition. It is rather like a reported experience of the late Mr. Melton Prior, the famous war correspondent. He dreamed twice that he saw himself shot and buried. His mother wrote to him, describing a similar dream, and imploring him not to go to the relief of Eshowe. He accordingly sent a substitute. In the engagement, the unfortunate substitute was one of the first men to be shot.[1] But this may have been a case of chance coincidence. Dreams are so numerous that some of them are sure to "hit on" by chance; and this was a very expectable kind of dream, in the circumstances. It is quite different, and much more evidential, when the premonition is conveyed in waking clairvoyance or other unusual state.

Mrs. Napier was lying in bed, awake, on a morning in July 1907. Suddenly the usual "magnetic" tinglings began. In a minute or two she seemed to find herself on a country road, and saw a wagon with three horses collide with a dog-cart:—

"Then from underneath the wagon I saw a man pull out a girl and a bicycle. I felt that this girl was my sister, though I could not see her very well. Then I recovered normal consciousness.

"Soon afterwards my sister came up with my breakfast, and I told her of my vision, asking her not to go

---

[1] *Daily Chronicle*, Nov. 3, 1910.

out cycling that day. It happened, however, that she particularly wanted a certain book from the neighbouring town-library, so I ultimately agreed to let her go, on her promising that if she saw a wagon with three horses, she would dismount and keep close to the hedge.

"She went. When about half-a-mile from the town, and riding up a hill, she saw before her a wagon with three horses. She immediately dismounted and walked close beside the hedge. Within a few seconds there was a sudden flash of lightning, and a scream from behind. Then a horse and trap dashed past—the horse had bolted, frightened by the lightning. But it was safely pulled up, and no one was hurt."

Mrs. Napier wrote out and sent me an account of this incident, three days after its occurrence. I have quoted from her letter, which lies before me. As she goes on to say, things did not turn out as seen; "but who knows what *might* have happened but for the warning?" [1]

"Chance-coincidence," says the sceptic. Well, perhaps so. But, knowing the frequency of Mrs. Napier's veridical experiences, and noting the amount of correct detail in many of them, I confess to a certain incredulity. "There is a point," as Mr. Lang has neatly said, "at which the explanations of common sense arouse scepticism."

Whether, in the case just described, Mrs. Napier's subliminal self somehow saw the

[1] I have the sister's written corroboration of the details. The case seems half-way between Mr. Prior's and Saul's (*Samuel* i. 10), though we can't admit the latter as "evidence" at this time of day.

danger ahead and communicated its knowledge to the upper levels by a vision of what might happen, or whether the warning came from external intelligences, no one can tell. Many interesting questions suggest themselves here, notably the question of the reality of Time. Is the Future really, to some higher Intelligences or to the hidden part of our own minds, *Present?* But that subject is too large, and too metaphysical, to be entered on here.[1]

In the next chapter we proceed a step further in the direction indicated by Mrs. Napier's phenomena. These latter are always spontaneous, and are not in the least under her control. Indeed, she manifests a rather unexpected inability to produce anything by trying—except a little automatic writing—for she cannot even get a rap or a tilt out of a table, though she has tried most perseveringly; and this is the more surprising as she has had occasional experiences (raps audible to others and, on one or two occasions, movement of objects without discoverable cause) which suggest "physical mediumship." Some people, however, seem able to induce, or at least to encourage or facilitate, phenomena of various kinds; particularly trance phenomena, such as are now to be described.

[1] It is desirable to state that Mrs. Napier has read the MS. of this chapter, and certifies the account as correct.

CHAPTER III

REPORT OF TWO SITTINGS WITH MISS McDONALD [1]

On August 8, 1906, my friend Mr. Frank Knight called on Miss McDonald—a well-known medium—at her house in the West End of London, and asked for a sitting. Miss McDonald was engaged, and suggested another day; but Mr. Knight persisted, and the afternoon of the same day (the day of the call) was fixed on. Mr. Knight wandered about the neighbourhood until the appointment-time came, fearing to return to his temporary dwelling-place (with a married sister some miles away) lest the supposedly wily medium should put detectives on his track and should learn his identity. He gave no name or address to the medium, either at his first call or at the sitting; and, so far as he knew, he was as complete a stranger to her as she was to him. He had never sat with a medium before, was quite unknown in spiritualistic

[1] Not the true name. Mr. Knight, however, permits me to give the true name and address to any serious inquirer.

society—having only just before become interested in such matters—and his home was 200 miles distant from London.

This first sitting was almost a blank. The medium was not in good trim. But she got the names Wilfrid and Frank, which were correct. [F. K.'s name is Wilfrid Frank Knight, though he rarely uses the first Christian name.] A few "spirits" were described as present, but were not recognized. A great upheaval in F. K.'s life "ten years ago" was alluded to, but this statement did not correspond with fact. He was also informed that he ought to have been in the medical profession; this is an appropriate and "veridical" remark, but may be due to chance.

F. K. did not bespeak another sitting, but, on the same evening, he wrote to Miss McDonald suggesting it. The medium arranged for the day but one following—*i. e.* August 10.

I give below, with F. K.'s kind permission, his own account of this sitting, almost exactly as written out in a letter to me on August 13, 1906. We discussed it together on his return home, and he has also carefully read the MS. of this chapter. There seems to be nothing to add thereto, and nothing therein to alter. Notes in square brackets are for the reader's information; round brackets contain remarks made at the time.

The medium borrowed my watch as before, held it to her forehead, and after some twisting of the features said "I see Henry." [My father's name was Henry. In reply to my inquiry she gave me the following further details.] "He died very suddenly—perhaps accident. Age about 30 to 32. Light brown hair, blue eyes, moustache, short beard. Broad-minded and better developed spiritually than most men passing over."

[My father died very suddenly through the bursting of a blood-vessel. His age was 31. The other details are probably correct.]

When Miss McDonald had reached this stage she slowly put out her hand towards me, her eyes meanwhile being closed. I said "Do you wish to shake hands with me?" To this she replied, in broken English, without any trace of her usual Scotch accent:—

"Yes, I always like to shake hands with the sitters of my medium. I was here when you called on Wednesday, but I could not see into your life so I did not attempt to speak. Now I must look around, but first I must tell you that spirit-life is a great reality, and that the spirits on both sides of the grave are alike children of the same great Father.

"Your life is at present all dark and tangled, but a great light is about to come into it, which will be like the rising of a beautiful evening star, and life will be all changed for you."

(Will this happen soon?)

"Yes—even now it is coming, and I am saying all this to prepare your mind for the great light that will soon dawn upon you. But I will now look into your life. When you were a little boy something happened which darkened your life. You were about six years old when some one very nearly related to you passed over, and your life was changed from what it should have been. There was a great financial change, and you could not become a medical man, as you ought to have done. Then when you went to school you were a very shy boy, and had much trouble with your schoolfellows, who did not understand you at all, but by mixing with the world since you have to a great extent thrown this off.

"You will excuse me, please, but I must go forward now to about six or eight months ago. Then a great trouble came into your life, and it became all dark. You were much troubled with business matters."

(Possibly, but there was no financial difficulty.)

"No, no, the trouble is connected with a person."

(Yes.)

"A lady."

(Yes, can you tell me anything about this lady? I should like to hear about her.)

"You would have married her."

(No, I should not.)

"I will look again. Lady, 55 to 57 years of age, brown hair, I hear Frederica."

(No.)

"It is Fre . . . something."

(Freda possibly?)

"Yes, yes, Freda, Freda [then in a faint voice] your other name . . . Katherine, Katherine."

As these words were spoken, Miss McDonald's head fell back a little, her eyes were closed, and she was very pale. She looked very much as if she had fainted, and appeared to be quite unconscious. In a few seconds her lips began to move again, and I detected my own name, Frank. Then louder and more distinctly until it ended in a delighted cry: "Frank! Frank!! Frank!!! Oh, my boy, my boy, my dear, dear boy." With a face shining with delight the medium seized my hand and pressed it in both hers:—

"Oh, my boy, my boy, I am not dead, I am not dead."

Then she began stroking my hands and face and hair, just as my mother used to do when we were talking together at night in her later invalid-days when I sat and chatted by her bedside before going to bed myself. The characteristic action was unmistakable.

"My dear boy, I never thought I could have got so near to you. God bless you, my love."

(Are all the others with you, mother?)

"Yes. All. All. Grandmother and Benjamin—and Benjamin too."

(Do you love me still?)

"Oh, yes, my dear, dear boy; I love you more than I can tell. I wish I could take you into my arms."

(And you know I love you, don't you?)

"I know, I know you do. I never knew until after I died how much you love me."

(Oh, mother, I would give my life to be with you. I am so very lonely.)

[Here I broke down. The hands continued their soft stroking of my face and hair, and the voice went on :—]

"Don't grieve, my dear lad, it is all for the best, Frank. God is good, God is so good. I love you, my dear, dear boy, and shall always be with you, and I will write you a little letter with your own hand, when you get home. My dear love to Janet—Janet and Herbert—and Herbert."

(Are you satisfied with us, and the lives we are living?)

"Yes."

(Am I to continue to keep my house on, and live as I am doing?)

"Yes, at present."

(Have you any special message for me?)

"God bless you, my dear, dear boy. God bless you. I shall be often with you."

The last words were very faint, and then, as they finished, the medium fell back in her chair, apparently unconscious. Soon, she began to come round with a series of twitchings, eventually opening her eyes and rubbing them.

"Do you feel all right?" I asked.

"Yes, right now, thank you. But I am sure I have been controlled by some other spirit as well as 'Sunbeam.' Did 'Sunbeam' speak to you?"

I gathered that she referred to the control with the broken English. Miss McDonald confirmed this, and said that it was a rare thing for "Sunbeam" to allow a strange spirit to control. Miss McDonald assured me that she had no consciousness of what had passed. I told her something of what had happened, and expressed myself satisfied with the sitting. We were leaving the room together, when Miss McDonald said :—

"Just wait a moment, I believe your grandmother is in the room. She is a little lady. Stoops rather. Was very active, while in the flesh. Wore a cap, and had brown hair in front, but I can see a little white behind. She had bright blue eyes, and her message to you is : 'I'm not old any more, Frank ! ' "

This ended the sitting.

[Notes on the details, by F. K.

It is true that I was "about six years old" when some one nearly related to me (my father) passed over. The remarks about my shyness as a boy, and the painful time I had at school, are specially applicable. I had to be taken away from the school, to prevent breakdown in health—the incipient illness being caused by the roughness of boarding-school life acting on a too sensitive organization.

The trouble "six or eight months ago" was, no doubt, my mother's death, which had occurred on Dec. 13, 1905—*i. e.* eight months previous to the sitting. She had been an invalid for many years, and the relations between us had been exceptionally intimate and tender. Her death truly left my life a blank. My brother and sister are married, and I live alone, so far as relatives are concerned.

My mother's age at death was 57. Name, Freda Katherine, as given by the control. Hair brown.

"Benjamin" was my uncle—mother's brother—who lived with us until his death in 1903.

Janet and Herbert are the names of my sister and brother.

I never told the medium where I came from, and at the first sitting she did not know my name. Naturally, I carefully refrained from mentioning any names of relatives, and I hardly think there had been time, between the two sittings, for any satisfactory detective work, even if the medium had succeeded in discovering what town I lived in, down in Yorkshire.

The description of my grandmother is peculiarly accurate as to the hair. She wore a brown *wig*, which did not always stay on quite straight, and sometimes allowed the grey to show. The other details are also correct. A frequent remark of hers was : " I'm an old, old woman, Frank."]

[General comments, by F. K.

When I entered Miss McDonald's drawing-room, I was an entire disbeliever, not only in " spirit-return " but also in survival. The sitting had a profound effect upon me; and during its progress, at all events, I had not the slightest doubt that I was actually speaking to my dead mother.

The sudden personation was very startling and dramatic, and, with the realistic cry, " Frank, Frank, my boy, my boy," certainly carried me away a little; but I did not lose control of my observing and reasoning faculties, and I am prepared to maintain the accuracy of this record in every essential detail.]

CHAPTER IV

SITTINGS WITH THE CLAIRVOYANT WATSON

The following five chapters describe some interesting sittings which took place at the house of a friend of mine. The medium is a "normal clairvoyant" who sees "spirit forms," describing them, giving names and various identifying details, and sometimes obtaining a considerable amount of impressional or automatic script. Notes were taken at each sitting, and the full account was written out as soon as possible (always within a day or two, at most) and was read and checked by one or more of the other sitters. A full report of each sitting was always given to me within a few days of its occurrence, and was discussed by me with one or more of those who had been present. I quote from these records. My MS. has been carefully read, and is approved as accurate, by the two principal sitters.

The medium is known to me and to others among my friends. None of these latter are spiritualists. Yet they are of opinion that the medium is honest, and has some kind of supernormal faculty. I myself have sat with him, with results to be mentioned later on. I started out with the usual suspicions of an "orthodox psychical researcher" (if such a contradiction in terms be permissible), but am now pretty thoroughly convinced of the medium's honesty. We have entirely failed to discover any indication of fraud, or indeed anything the least to his discredit. I believe him to be a man of integrity, and the other sitters coincide in this opinion.

The chief sitter in the following series was Mr. Frank Knight, whose sittings with Miss McDonald have just been described. He is a hard-headed business man of about thirty-five years of age. The other principal sitter was Mr. Isaac Oddy, a well-known composer. I have altered the true names, for, though my friends would have permitted their use, there is so much ignorant prejudice against these matters that it seems better to hide identities, particularly as in this case the true names would lead to the recognition of other people mentioned in the sittings, who might reasonably object to publicity.

Mr. Knight and Mr. Oddy were, at the beginning of their investigations, vigorous Haeckelians; but their results have led them to adopt conclusions approximately the same as those expressed by Myers in his great work, *Human Personality*. Both of them have keen minds, of the legal type; quick to detect flaws in the evidence, drastic in their methods, persistent in their demands for proof. Mr. Knight is now a member of the S.P.R., and Mr. Oddy also is in full sympathy with its work and its methods.

The medium (Watson) is a man of about thirty. His usual procedure is to sit with a small table before him, on which are paper and pencil. The sitters are grouped in semicircle to his right and left. He often describes the "influence" which he gets from each sitter, correctly diagnosing the state of each one's health, or hitting off their occupations or special interests. But the best feature of his mediumship is the description of "spirit forms," with names and messages which he seems to get by a kind of inner hearing; though the automatic script is interesting, and often important, and has the advantage of furnishing a first-hand record of the messages.

So far as can be ascertained, all the sitters were unknown to Watson at the beginning of the sittings. He knew Mr. Knight's name, the latter having written to him asking for a sitting, but they had not met before. He assured F. K. that he knew nothing about him except that he (F. K.) was a bachelor. The latter is not a prominent man in public affairs, being very much of a reader and student; and his name does not appear in the title of his firm. It seems probable enough that the medium's assertion was true. Mr. Knight of course did not mention his sittings with Miss McDonald, and was careful to give no information about his family or his affairs generally.

Sitting 1.

Oct. 5, 1906. Watson had called on F. K. to arrange about sittings.

Whilst talking about these arrangements, Watson said that he felt the strong influence of the spirit of a lady, who was present in the room. This lady was of middle age (the exact age—57—was given in Sitting 3) and her name was Mary Katherine. [Partly correct, for F. K.'s mother; the true name is Freda Katherine Knight, as given in full as signature to a letter in Sitting 4.]

F. K. asked for further information. Watson rested his hand on F. K.'s knee—the only time that physical contact occurred between medium and sitter—and proceeded as below:—

"The spirit of your mother is present. I feel her influence, but cannot see her. She is greatly devoted to you. She impresses me very strongly. She wishes to give you a test of her actual presence. Do you see anything written on the table?" (No.)[1] "*I* do; I see a name. It is the name of some relative of yours who died many years ago. The name is Oliver Upton. This gentleman is not present now, but your mother knows that you will recognize the name."

[Oliver Upton, born 1784, died 1856, was F. K's. maternal great-grandfather.]

"Your mother is now taking me away from here—I am at Queen Street Station, Z——. I am following her body to the grave, through the streets of Z—— out into the suburbs, where her body lies with that of a gentleman.

"She is very anxious you should know that though her body is in the grave, her spirit is here with you now."

[F. K.'s mother was buried at St. James's Church, in a suburb of Z——, where his father and infant sister also lie. She—Mrs. K.—was taken for burial, by train from X—— (the town of the sitting), via Queen Street Station, Z——.]

The medium went on to say that he also received an impression that the lady in question, as she lay dying, had had two thoughts specially in mind. One was surprise that death was so near; the other was conjecture as to where she would be buried.

[It is impossible to verify this. The notions were not present in F. K.'s mind, but he says that the statement is quite likely to be true. His mother's death was unexpected, the doctor's verdict having been more favourable; and her mind would quite possibly be occupied with the place of burial, as many of her

[1] Round brackets contain remarks made at the time, by the sitters. Square brackets contain elucidatory comments for the reader. See Appendix for genealogical table of Mr. Knight's connections.

blood-relations are buried at X—— (where she died, and where F. K. lives), while her husband and one child lie at Z——, forty miles away.]

[General comments by F. K.

It might be possible for a fraudulent medium to obtain many of these details by inquiry. It is, however, very unlikely that the name of my great-grandfather, Oliver Upton, could have been so obtained. It is fifty-one years since he died, and there is no obvious link to connect me with him.]

SITTING 2.

Oct. 19, 1906. *Present, F. K., I. O., a Mr. H. H., and medium.*

After being in the room a few minutes, the medium had the impression that a previous tenant of the house had died there, after a long illness. [All present denied this; but it was afterwards found to be true of a Mr. Charles Underwood. Mr. Oddy, however, remembered afterwards that he must have known of it, so telepathy from his mind is not excluded, though it does not follow that such a supposition would be the true one, even if the more obvious one of fraud be excluded.]

The sitters then sat round a small table.

Turning to Mr. Oddy, the medium said that he got from him a strong influence of music. He also described spirit forms associated with him, and obtained the maiden name of his mother. I omit the details, as they were not noted at the time, being supplied by Mr. Oddy afterwards. The medium then turned to Mr. Knight and said:—

"I see standing between you and the next gentleman"—Mr. H.—"the figure of a lady. She has brown hair, brushed up high, and straight back from her forehead—brown eyes—about 36 years of age—her name is Kathleen." (Any other name?) "Yes, Upton." (Any other name?) "Not at present."

Later, while talking to I. O., the medium suddenly remarked:—

"There's some one calling out *Thornes, Thornes.* It is the lady—her name is Kathleen Upton Thornes.

"She has with her—holding her by the hand—a man about 51 years of age—in a weakly, tottering condition, whose mind was afflicted while he lived. His name is Benjamin Thornes, and he is the brother of the lady called Kathleen." (Any other name?) "No, not at present."

Then, a little later—:

"I have got the other name you wanted. It is C-A-R-T-E-R,—Carter. The correct names are Kathleen Upton Thornes and Benjamin Carter Thornes, and they are blood-relations of Mr. Knight."

The names and descriptions are correct. The people in question were F. K.'s aunt and uncle respectively, who lived and died at his old home, not the house in which he now lives. Kathleen Thornes died in 1889, aged 39. Benjamin Thornes died in 1903, aged 51.

[Comment by F. K.

The descriptive detail preceded the names, and I recognized the personalities described, before the names were mentioned.

The names Upton and Carter are family names, but they were not used by the Thornes's either in correspondence or conversation. I very much doubt whether any one outside my immediate family had heard the name Carter associated with me, as that branch of the Carters has been extinct for about 100 years, and they did not at any time live in this district.]

CHAPTER V

SITTINGS WITH WATSON (*continued*)

SITTING 3.

Nov. 16, 1906. *Present, F. K., I. O., two or three of their friends, and the medium. The principal details, however, concern the usual two sitters.*

THE medium began by saying that the sitters had been wrong in asserting at the last sitting that no one had died in the house. He said that the spirit of the man who had died there had appeared to him in the railway carriage as he was returning home after the sitting.

This spirit was now in the room. He appeared as an elderly, bearded man, and gave his name as Charles Underwood. He was waiting in these regions in expectation of some event which would take place soon.

[Kenelm Underwood, the previous tenant of F. K.'s house, and son of Charles Underwood, died about three months after the date of this sitting. His death had long been expected. Apparently—on the *primâ facie* supposition—the father had come to meet his dying son.]

The medium then took paper and pencil, and wrote the figures "1875." Turning to F. K., he said :—

"The spirit of your sister is in the room. She died in 1875. [Correct.] She was under three months old when she died [correct], but now I see her looking like a beautiful woman of thirty." [Cf. Sitting 4.] "Her name is Nora. [Correct.] She is often with you.

"Her father is also in the room—a fine healthy-looking man. His name is Henry, and he died in 1880, at Uppertown, Z——, I think. [All correct. Uppertown is a suburb of the town Z——, forty miles from X——.]

"The lady whose portrait is hanging on the wall [F. K.'s mother] is also present, in fact hers is the strongest influence in the room; and she has brought the other people with her, so that you may recognize them.

"There is a well-built, well-dressed man of about 52 years of age standing on the hearthrug now. He was a shrewd business man, and you [to F. K.] have a good deal to do with his widow in business, and see her very often. He has brown hair, and his name is Kenneth Frederic." [All correct, as applied to F. K.'s deceased uncle, with whose widow F. K. is associated in business affairs. Cf. Sittings 4 and 6.]

Later, the medium remarked that he saw an old lady wearing a black silk shawl. A relative of Mr. Knight, and was over 80 when she died. Her name was Theresa, and there was something in the room near to him (the medium) which used to belong to her.

[These facts apply to F. K.'s grandmother, whose name was Theresa Carter Thornes. Cf. Sitting 4. She often wore a black silk shawl; and her Bible, used regularly by her for over twenty years, was on the shelf at the medium's elbow, though he did not know this.]

The medium then stated that he was being taken by F. K.'s mother to the house in which she died, which was only a short distance away. From there he was taken to the station, and forward to Z——. Coming out of Queen Street Station he turned sharply to the right, and straight up a long road, upon which trams were moving backward and forward. As the suburbs were reached he saw a succession of large houses surrounded by gardens and trees. At last he turns to the left, going a short distance up a road which has large houses on one side, and open fields on the other. A little way up this road, he comes to a churchyard gate. Here he stops an instant, and is then taken forward to a spot on the right-hand side of the church, where he sees a number of large white stones, such as are seen on rockeries. Here he is left.

[Comment by F. K.

This is a remarkably accurate description of the route from Queen Street Station to St. James's Church, and the white rockery-stones are actually on the grave.]

In connection with Mr. Oddy, a tall gentleman of about seventy years of age was described. He was stated to be a relative, to wear a beard and moustache, and to have a prominent nose. Name, Joseph Oddy.

[Joseph Oddy is the name of I. O.'s deceased grandfather. Cf. Sitting 8.]

The medium then wrote the names "Bertha Oddy—Joseph Oddy—Peace." The "Peace" seemed to confuse him, and he could not tell what was meant. As a matter of fact, "Peace" was the name of Joseph Oddy's wife.

Later, the medium felt the very strong influence of a relative of I. O.'s on his father's side. He complained that this relative, who was apparently a great-uncle and who had passed away many years ago, was endeavouring to hypnotize him. He also accurately described several of I. O.'s relatives who live in a distant town, but I omit these details, as the persons' names were not obtained. Descriptions, unless very specific and containing some marked characteristic, are not the best of evidence, though they are sometimes striking enough to serve as useful corroboration.

[Comment by F. K.

I do not believe that any one in our town, outside our small family circle, knew that I had had a sister Nora, who died in infancy, in 1875. This incident seems to me rather good.]

Sitting 4.

Dec. 12, 1906. *Present, F. K. and medium only, until near the end, when F. K.'s brother and sister-in-law (Mr. and Mrs. Herbert Knight) came in.*

After some general conversation, the medium said:—

"Your mother is in the room—I can see her very plainly. She tells me that it is just a year to-day since she passed away. [Correct.] Why, your family must be nearly all dead! I can see quite a lot of them. I see two men and three women of your mother's family. [Correct.] Besides a man of your own age or a little younger, named Henry. [Applies correctly to F. K.'s father at time of his death.]

At this point the medium took paper and pencil, and wrote:—

"Dear Son,—I am delighted for this opportunity. I have been endeavouring to make you aware of my presence early this morning. At 7 minutes to 8 o'clock to-day do you remember any particular sensation, because I was in close touch with you then. [Note A.]

"Your father and I are happily re-united after so long a separation. Twenty-five years seemed a long time, but now one understands the experiences of life better. [Note B.]

"My sister Kathleen is indeed engaged in work that would be pleasant to any good soul. Would you know that Florence as well and I have all come together, and what a greeting it was. You would perhaps know how soon she followed your little sister Nora. Well, she has been her guardian and teacher, and such a beautiful woman she is now. [Note C.]

"Oh! the beauty of this fuller life. I cannot express it to you, Frank, but I hope to give you personally some evidence of my continued affection for you. I hope to make myself tangible to you as soon as is possible.

"Your grandmother, my own dear mother, is now quite consciously united to us all.

"Quite a charming circle we make.

"I cannot say more. My time is spent in this direction. Don't think of me as being in St. James's, but as being near you often.

"Your dear mother,

"FREDA KATHERINE KNIGHT."

[Correct, F. K.'s mother.]

At this point, Mr. and Mrs. Herbert Knight came into the room. The medium proceeded to give his impressions, addressing H. K., to whom they did not apply. To F. K., however, they did apply :—

"There is a gentleman now present in the room about 53 years of age, well dressed, and giving the impression of a prosperous man with commercial interests, a determined character and of a somewhat critical mind.

"His name was Frederic or Ferdinand, and he has a son still living." [Cf. Sitting 6, p. 55.]

"He is much interested in a certain business which is at present carried on by a lady—his widow. The business requires to be carefully watched in certain details, and certain proposed extensive outlays must be avoided, as they are unnecessary.

"Matters, however, will soon right themselves. With Frederic is a man called Nathan, who passed away at least 36 years ago, aged about 45. [See Note D.]

"There is also present the old lady over 80, previously described, and she is still wearing the black silk shawl. With her is another old lady, wearing a very antique dress, and a crinoline."

F. K. asked for their names, and the medium wrote :—

"Theresa Carter and Nora her mother." [Correct Christian names of F. K.'s grandmother, Theresa Carter Thornes, *née* Upton, and her mother, Nora Upton.]

It was then stated by the medium that Frederic, Nathan, and Theresa Carter were all interested in the business at Stanbury. [This business, with which F. K. is now associated, was the property of these three persons successively, and they are the only deceased members of the family who have had any connection with it.] [1]

Then came the following written communication:—

"I am Grandmother Thornes. I am so glad. Just have patience. All things come to those who wait. That difficulty is easily got over. It is Kenneth Ferdinand. Just take the advice."

[Should be Kenneth Frederic, for F. K.'s uncle.]

"I am your Aunt Florence. Thirty years since I left my earthly home. Dear Boy." [F. K. here asked if the full name could be given.] "Yes. My name was Florence Brown—Thornes." [Cf. Sitting 8, p. 66.]

Benjamin Thornes was again described as groping forward, and as having suffered from mental affliction. [Cf. Sitting 2, p. 41.] Also as being about 50 years old, which was also the age at which Kenneth Frederic died. The medium felt that there was a tie of relationship between them. [They were brothers, and each died in his 52nd year.]

[Notes by F. K.

(A) At 7 minutes to 8 on the morning of the sitting, I was standing in my bedroom, saying aloud (just after glancing at my watch) that if my mother could hear my voice, I wanted her to know that the medium was coming in the evening, and would she, if

[1] Cf., for a spirit's continued interest in an earthly business, Sir Oliver Lodge's Report in *Proceedings S.P.R.*, Part 58, pp. 168, 193.

possible, write me a letter through his hand. I was not, however, conscious of any particular sensation.

(B) My father died in 1880, my mother in 1905. The " twenty-five years " is therefore correct.

(C) " Kathleen " was my aunt — my mother's sister. [Cf. Sitting 2, p. 41.]

Florence Brown (*née* Thornes) was another maternal aunt, who died in 1876. My little sister Nora died in 1875, so the statement that Florence " followed " her soon, is correct.

(D) My uncle, Kenneth Frederic Thornes, died in 1895, aged 51.

The business with which I am connected is now carried on by his widow. Certain extensive outlays *were* actually being contemplated at the time, and I am convinced that no one living, except the members of the firm and myself, knew anything whatever concerning the proposals which were under consideration. The advice given has turned out, in the light of recent events, to be very sound.

The phraseology of the letter purporting to be from my mother, is not always what I should have expected from her; but, on any hypothesis, the medium's personality may be assumed to colour the messages somewhat.]

CHAPTER VI

SITTINGS WITH WATSON (*continued*)

SITTING 5.

Feb. 22, 1907. *Present, F. K., Mr. and Mrs. Herbert Knight, Mr. I. Oddy, a Mr. Newman (friend of F. K. and I. O.), Miss T. (F. K.'s housekeeper) and medium.*

THE medium told Mrs. Herbert Knight that he saw with her a gentleman, about 44 years old. He had done a lot of writing when living—was in fact a journalist. Asked for the name, the medium got " Wilfrid Renton." Had passed away prematurely, and with great reluctance, being at the time engaged in important work, and being also loath to leave his wife and children. This spirit was waiting for something to happen towards which he was looking with much interest.

[Note by F. K.

Wilfrid Renton was Mrs. H. K.'s father. He was a journalist, and he died aged 44. At the time of the sitting, his eldest son (William) was very ill, dying about two months afterwards, on April 9. A e tl the father

 51ppar n y

was waiting for his son, as in the Charles Underwood case described in Sitting 3, p. 43.]

Immediately afterwards, the medium said that he felt himself to be taken a long railway journey. Arrived at a small village in Northamptonshire. [About 100 miles from place of sittings.] Some one lives there with whom Mrs. Herbert Knight occasionally comes in contact. The medium got the name of the village as Oundle, and the name of the family as Hanby. Later, he got the name Thomas Hanby.

[Note by F. K.

Mrs. H. K.'s maternal grandfather was Thomas Hanby, and he lived at Oundle, Northamptonshire. Mrs. H. K. did not remember his Christian name, but on inquiry it was found to have been Thomas.]

Mr. Newman, who had never seen the medium before, and who so far as is ascertainable was not known to him, was correctly given his father's name (surname and three baptismal names) and the age at which he died; also his own profession (teacher). [Mr. Newman's name was not mentioned by the sitters, and he was not introduced to the medium.]

A deceased relative of I. O.'s was named and described, and F. K.'s father and mother were also said to be present.

At this sitting, the new evidential matter is not large in quantity, but it is good in quality. It is not likely that the medium possessed normally-acquired knowledge of the name and place of residence of Mrs. Herbert Knight's grandfather. Further, good evidential matter was given to Mr. Newman, who, so far as we know, was a stranger to the medium.

SITTING 6.

April 18, 1907. *Present, F. K., I. O., Mr. Newman, Mr. H., and Mr. B. (friends of F. K. and I. O.).*

The medium described and named correctly a relative of I. O.'s. He then went on to refer to another deceased relative of I. O., describing but not naming her. The description was recognized. There was said to be in this lady's home circle a girl who was not at all well, and who would require strict attention. [Afterwards verified.] With the exception of the head of the house, all the members of this family were girls. [Correct.] The young lady who appeared, and who had died after a short illness, was said to be buried in a flat churchyard where there are many other graves; there was stated to be a very white stone over her grave. [This about the grave is quite wrong; I quote it in order that the total evidentiality may not seem stronger than it is. In the whole series, the number of inaccurate statements is remarkably small. I quote them all. Where I *omit* incidents, they are evidential and tend to strengthen the case; being omitted here as being likely to confuse the reader by introducing other names, or for some similar reason. The total evidential mass is therefore greater, and not less, than that of the account here printed.]

A young man was described as connected with Mr. Newman. Very energetic, well educated, studious, but business-like. Had died prematurely, leaving a wife and some children. [Correct, of Mr. N.'s father. Cf. Sitting 5.] One of his children, who died in infancy, had predeceased him. [Wrong.] The medium then gave the name, correctly as far as given, but omitting one Christian name. [The full name had been correctly given in Sitting 5, p. 52.] A correct description of the churchyard and grave was also given.

A spirit was described for Mr. H., but was not recognized. Correct statements were made regarding Mr. H.'s health and business position. Full notes were not taken.

A spirit was described for Mr. B., but was not recognized.

Standing beside F. K., said the medium, was a well-made man who had died 12 years previously. Age perhaps 54. High brow, full face, grey mixture suit—a well-groomed man. Had been much engrossed in business, and shortly before he died had had much business worry which had no doubt hastened his end.

After much difficulty, the medium got the name Kenneth Frederic Thornes. Was much interested in the business with which F. K. is connected, and certain advice was given to the latter concerning it, though it was stated that there were others living who were more nearly concerned than F. K. [True.] These persons, however, could not be reached by the communicator. [They are not interested in psychical research, and are in fact hostile to the subject.]

[Note by F. K.

My uncle, Kenneth Frederic Thornes, died in March 1895. "Twelve years ago" is therefore correct. He had much business worry, shortly before he died, owing to the destruction of a mill by fire. The worry incidental to rebuilding, and loss of trade, affected his health, and the illness from which he died developed at this time.]

The medium then gave a description of an old lady, apparently F. K.'s grandmother. Name, Theresa.

Later, he turned to F. K. and asked if his brother (Mr. Herbert Knight) knew about the sitting; for he (the medium) had caught a sudden impression of Mr. and Mrs. H. K. standing behind F. K. The lady's eyes appeared to be inflamed.

[Note by F. K.

We noted the time of this last statement—9.25 p.m. At the conclusion of the sitting, my brother (H. K.) came into the room. Until we saw him we were unaware that he was in the house. He had entered quietly, and had stood by the door of the room in which the sitting was being held. He put his ear to the closed door to catch, if possible, what was being said. The first words he heard were those of the medium when he asked if my brother knew of the sitting. The time was 9.25.

It appeared that Mrs. H. K. was suffering that evening from headache and inflamed eyes owing to a trying bicycle ride, against wind and dust, in the afternoon. She therefore stayed at home instead of coming to my house with my brother. The sitters knew nothing of this until informed by H. K., and there is no reason to suppose that the medium had any normally-acquired knowledge of it.]

CHAPTER VII

SITTINGS WITH WATSON (*continued*)

SITTING 7.

June 12, 1907. *Present, F. K., I. O., and medium. Towards the end, there came in Mr. Herbert Knight and his wife's sister—Miss Renton, of Y——, thirty miles away.*

THE medium told F. K. that there was some difficulty and confusion in connection with his (F. K.'s) domestic affairs, and that if this matter was not faced at once it would be more difficult to face later on.

[Correct, and peculiarly appropriate; but the details are too private to quote here, another person being involved to whom injury or pain might be caused if the identities were discovered. It seems to me, knowing all the facts, that any normally-acquired knowledge of the state of affairs, on the part of the medium, is improbable to the point of incredibility.[1] Later in the sitting, an automatically-written message was produced,

[1] F. K. is very sure that no one except himself and perhaps his brother can have known anything about the situation—which was an altogether peculiar one, and not a matter of finances.

in which this same matter was alluded to. The message purported to come from F. K.'s mother. The wording was exactly appropriate to the situation, yet had a curiously purposeful-seeming indefiniteness, as if the communicator were deliberately choosing phrases which, though intelligible enough to F. K., should nevertheless give no clear impression to an outsider—*e. g.* the medium.

Some automatic script was next produced, purporting to come from the Kenelm Underwood of Sitting 3, Chapter V. It was dramatic, unexpected in matter and style (therefore inexplicable by telepathy from the sitters' consciousnesses) and somewhat evidential; but it involves family matter of a private nature, and I suppress it lest it should cause pain to certain living relatives.

Early in this sitting the medium got the impression of a young lady who had been associated with F. K. some time ago. Not much over 30 when she died. Name, Stonor. With her, and related to her, was an old gentleman, somewhat feeble, over 70 when he died. Name, George Stonor. Had been neighbours of F. K.'s at a former address. F. K.'s mother, Freda Knight, "had given them financial assistance at a time of great trouble."

[Note by F. K.

The above names, descriptions, ages, and facts, are correct. The financial help was given through the doctor in attendance on the Stonors (father and daughter) in order that they should not know its source. They were our next-door neighbours at a former address, and they died there, in 1901, within a few weeks of each other. It seems extremely unlikely that the medium could have learnt the fact of the money help, in any ordinary way. So far as I am aware, no one ever knew of the incident except the Stonors, the doctor, my mother, and myself. I had not thought of it for a long time, as it was a small matter, and occurred so long ago. I do not think I had ever heard Mr. Stonor's Christian name, but I find on visiting the cemetery and looking up the tombstone, that it was George, as stated. His age at death was 73, his daughter's 32.]

The medium then announced that F. K.'s mother was again present, whereupon F. K. asked that she would give him a test of her identity by telling him something which was not in his own knowledge, but which could be verified by some relative or friend. The following was written at once:—

"I am thinking of what you suggest, and I will in the meantime think of something.

"You would perhaps not remember something that happened to Benjamin when he was twelve years old.

"How I can tell you I don't know, but I will try—Poor boy—He is all right now [pause].

"Herbert is all right I think, but [pause] when you were born, let me see, I almost think it was at Uppertown, but, oh dear! how strange. It is like going into a strange country, going back to those times. I visited the grave where I am supposed to be buried. It is very nice. The stones are still there. Dear me, I feel quite a dual personality. More I cannot say now. I feel used up, or rather to have absorbed all at my command for the present.

"Don't feel the least afraid. *God is not mocked.* I am your mother. Her care is still yours. Love."

[Note by F. K.

I believe my Uncle Benjamin was bitten by a horse when he was a boy.

I was born at Uppertown, Z——.

The "stones" are still on the grave.

The communicator apparently was wandering from one idea to another in a dream-like condition of mind.]

To Miss Renton, the medium made the following statements :—

That her health was not good. That she was passing through a period of great strain and had done a lot of nursing recently. That she was at present nursing a lady, her mother, whose health was very precarious. They must at once leave their present home, which could never be the same to them again. Her mother's life depended on this removal. [Note by J. A. H., Nov. 17, 1910. They have not removed. Mrs. Renton is still alive, though in poor health.]

Miss Renton asked where they were to go, and the medium at once wrote the following:—

"Tell your mother to go home to the old country in Northamptonshire for a little while. It will do her a heap of good. Time will bring much change, but all has happened best, for suffering cannot bring happiness. Rest at last. W. R."

[Miss Renton's brother, William Renton, had died at home, of consumption, on April 9—*i. e.* two months before the sitting. Probably he is the ostensible communicator, though the initial letters W. R. might also stand for Wilfrid Renton, Miss Renton's father, who died a few years before. See p. 51.]

The medium then stated that he saw, connected with Miss Renton, a well-dressed gentleman, middle-aged, a clear speaker, related to her through her father. Had died since the latter. Name, Thomas.

[This applies correctly to Miss Renton's deceased uncle, Thomas Renton.]

A lady also was seen. Had lived in a farming district a long way off. Had been dead a long time, and inquiry concerning her should be made among old relatives. Name, Mary Hanby.

[Mary Hanby turns out to have been the name of Miss Renton's great-grandmother, who died long ago in a Northamptonshire village. At the sitting, Miss Renton disputed the name, but the medium stuck to his guns.]

[Note by F. K.

Miss Renton was not expected at the sitting; had come from Y—— (30 miles away) with her mother during the afternoon; and had never seen the medium before. Yet every statement made to her was correct. At the time, she thought the name Mary should be "Martha" to be applicable; but inquiry proved the former to be correct.]

For Mr. Herbert Knight the medium described a woman of thirty, name Edna. [Unrecognized. A deceased aunt of H. K.'s, however, had a name very like Edna. Perhaps this was what was intended.]

CHAPTER VIII

SITTINGS WITH WATSON (*continued*)

SITTING 8.

July 5, 1907. *Present, F. K., I. O., and medium.*

The medium complained at the opening of the sitting that he was not feeling well. Perhaps this may account for the mixed results. The influence apparently was constantly changing, and many of the messages and descriptions were disjointed and incomplete. In spite, however, of much confusion, some interesting results were obtained.

The medium got the name Fanny, connected with I. O. The name belonged to some one rather past middle age, who had been dead a few years.

Later, he wrote :—

"Fanny Oddy. My ambitions have been quite realized."

I. O. inquired where she had died.

"Grey Gables." [Incorrect. "Grey Gables" is I. O.'s house, but Fanny Oddy—I. O.'s aunt—did not die there.]

Asked where she was buried, the answer was "Storm Ridge," which is correct.

An old gentleman was then described—bearded, stooping, holding out before him a bundle of herbs. Was a connection of a young lady—related to Mr. Oddy—whose presence was felt, but whose name the medium could not get. Asked for the old man's name, Watson produced writing as below.

"That is my grandfather—K. M. I am your cousin." [Full name of K. M. was requested.] "Who passed away at Holywell ?" ["Well, who did ?" asked Mr. Oddy.] "Kenneth Mills." (Is this your grandfather ?) "Yes."

[Kenneth Mills was an herbalist who died near Holywell. He was the grandfather of I. O.'s cousin, who had purported to send messages before, and who apparently is the young lady whose presence the medium had felt.]

The name "Sarah Ann" was then written. [This was the name of the cousin's mother.] I. O. then asked where his cousin had died. "Southport" was written. [Wrong. She lived several years at Southport, but died at Blackpool.]

The influence then changed, and the following was written, apparently to F. K. from his mother :—

"My dear Boy,—Love to Herbert and yourself, not forgetting *Annie*. How strange it seems. What a concourse of us. I feel sorry about the vacant . . ." ["Annie" unrecognized: F. K.'s sister's name is Janet.]

Here the writing stopped abruptly, and the medium's attempts to continue the communication were unsuccessful. After waiting a few moments he wrote as below:—

"My dear Friend,—I would have you know the communications are mixed, by the reason of the young lady, the dark man's friend, and the lady of the house, both attempting at the same time to give a message. This is common enough as you are aware, and they are excited to no small degree. We will do our best to put them in order. Perhaps it will be more direct and consecutive afterwards. The fair man should really have a personal message soon, as the anxiety displayed in his part for a time makes their friends equally anxious. I am your old friend,

"THOMAS WARD."

F. K. is fair; I. O. dark. The sitting was being held as usual at the home of the former, so the "lady of the house" is correctly used if referring to F. K.'s mother. The "young lady, the dark man's friend," apparently purports to be I. O.'s cousin, already mentioned.

The medium remarked that "Thomas Ward" was well known to him as a frequent communicator. The name was not known to the sitters. The "old friend's" well-meant efforts, however, seemed to be ineffectual, for nothing further was received at this sitting, either from I. O.'s cousin or F. K.'s mother.

A communication apparently intended for I. O. was :—

"'Occupy till I come' is a passage of scripture which your grandfather gives you. J. O."

Mr. Oddy asked for his grandfather's name. "James." [Wrong.] "Joseph." [Right.]

The medium then described a young lady of about 30 years of age, wearing her hair brushed back. Asked for the name, he wrote "Florence B. Thornes." Asked for her married name, "Brown" was given. How long had she been dead? "Over 30 years." [All this is correct as to F. K.'s aunt. Cf. Sitting 4, p. 49.]

The following was then written :—

"I am anxious to give you some idea of the real life. I may be unknown personally to you, but your tastes and pursuits generally draw me into your surroundings. Music, the noblest science known to man, which angels honoured long ere time began, was my delight.

"Its sweet seraphic lays shall hand your memory down to future days.

"K. I. Garrison."

This was evidently intended for I. O., who, as I have said, is a well-known musician. While I. O. and F. K. were discussing the message, the medium began to write again :—

I took part along with you at an organ recital at some Meeting House some time ago, and I believe it was at Stanbury." [" Whereabout at Stanbury ? " asked I. O.] " Industry Street."

It happens to be a fact that I. O., a few months before the sitting, had given an organ recital at a place of worship in Industry Street, Stanbury (a few miles away), but he was not conscious of any assistance from " the other side " on that occasion !

"K. I. Garrison " is the name of a man who was organist at X—— Parish Church about 50 years ago. This fact was unknown to F. K., but I. O. had probably heard it, though he could not remember at the time anything about a K. I. Garrison, and had to ask his father, who was able to supply the information.

The medium also described a tall, elderly man, not very old, rather lean and grey, with a high brow, aquiline nose, and shaggy whiskers, dressed in a black cloth suit. Had probably been a preacher. The words " 14th chap. Cor." were written, and the medium inclined to think that the same communicator had written the message " Occupy till I come," etc.

The description would apply correctly to I. O.'s grandfather, Joseph Oddy.

The Kenneth Mills incident was perhaps

the best piece of evidence in this sitting, as it would have been difficult for a fraudulent medium to find out any connection between this man and Mr. Oddy. He was I. O.'s cousin's grandfather, but was not the grandfather of I. O. himself. *I. e.*, he was the cousin's *mother's* father, while I. O.'s relationship to the cousin was through the latter's father. Kenneth Mills was therefore not a blood-relation of I. O.

SITTING 9.

Aug. 23, 1907. *Present, F. K. and medium.*

The medium felt the influence of an old lady whom he had previously seen several times at these sittings. She was over 80 when she died, and had died at the same house as F. K.'s mother, but had predeceased her. She had not been dead long, however, when his mother [her daughter] followed her. She was of a very affectionate disposition, and had been specially fond of F. K., liked to have him about her, and would always be wanting to know what he was doing and where he was going.

[Note by F. K.

Correct, as to my grandmother, Theresa Carter Thornes. Cf. Sittings 3, 4, and 6, pp. 44, 48, 55.]

The medium then felt the strong influence of F. K.'s mother. He was impelled to say that the discipline to which F. K. had been subjected in his earlier days, when he had apparently had a rough time of it away from home, had been for his good.

The following writing was then produced :—

" My dear Boy,—What a pleasure it is to be able to write a line or two to you. It is very difficult to keep in line my mind while I give you a message. Were you yourself at all intuitive I have no doubt you would soon feel my presence, but time may bring this result yet. I can assure you I shall endeavour to my utmost to give you what is essential for your welfare spiritually.

" My object is to make clear to you my interest is still as strong as ever. I am sure you are happier already."

[Note by F. K.

I was standing over the medium while this writing was being produced, and I here interjected a request for something evidential—something about herself or my other relatives which I could verify by inquiry. The writing resumed as follows.]

" My brother Kenneth Frederic was in touch with me, and may possibly give you some idea of his presence soon. My dear child, were you able to comprehend the difficulty we have in bringing to you the evidence you so long for, you, I am sure, would not be so anxious."

[Here F. K. asked if she could complete the message about his Uncle Benjamin. See Sitting 7, p. 60.]

" You know Benjamin was a great charge for so long, but no longer does that obtain . . ."

(" Please tell me more about Benjamin.")]

" I cannot grasp your desire, it seems as though I get perplexed."

[F. K. again presses for evidence of identity. " Tell

me more about yourself. Whose daughter were you, for example ? "]

"Nathan Thornes'." [Correct.]

The writing then proceeded :—

"How puzzled I am. Dear me ! Probably it will come all right, but the means don't seem to come to my hand——"

[A pause. F. K. asked if she could remember any of the incidents in connection with her last illness.]

"As regards my suffering bodily I cannot speak, for I no longer retain the sensation." [A pause.] "Your thought sometimes is very clear to me, but I cannot for my life symbolize it to you, why, I cannot tell. I seem so near and yet so far, for the subtlety of the atmosphere prevents me perfecting it. I am sure you are anxious. What for I cannot just realize, but if you cannot feel me near I don't know what else to do. We are undoubtedly in close contact, but time and space is not brought into account. On wings of aspiration we commune and our manner of communication is kept up in this way."

[Here F. K. interrupted to ask if there was no way by which he could be made conscious of her presence, no little sign by which he might know she was with him.]

"With all your senses combined physically you are unable to see that your comprehension is but meagre relating to time and occupation and correspondence."

[F. K. had also asked what she did with her time, whether the others were with her, and how they communicated.]

"It is unity of mind here that brings us close, not so much blood ties, though we are as we were before, near together.

"Henry and I, though he seems quite ahead of me in many ways, is very near to me, and is ever impinging me with his knowledge. Your little sister—I say so because you would know her better—is truly a wise messenger, having been schooled in a superior plane of thought." [Pause.]

"I should like our grave to be kept in order, though

it does not follow its neglect would affect me, but you know my mind about it. It is far better to be in your mind than in the grave. I shall have to give it up this time. I shall not relax my efforts, though I don't know just what is wanted. Perhaps it will occur to me.

"My dear boy, you are still my charge, don't misunderstand me. I am so glad you are so happily fixed. Your place is like home.

"I must leave you,
"YOUR MOTHER."

No further writing was obtained, but the medium went on to describe a young man of medium height, rather fair, slight moustache, sunken cheeks, about 26 years of age, who had been dead about ten years, probably longer. Was associated with F. K. through some lady still living, but no name could be obtained, except the letter A, and what sounded to the medium like "Norton."

[Unrecognized.]

[At a later sitting, on January 8, 1908, a "Mrs. Norton" was referred to as a friend of F. K.'s maternal grandfather. This was given in response to requests for a test answer. F. K. knew nothing of a Mrs. Norton, but, on questioning an old man who had known his (F. K.'s) maternal grandfather and grandmother, he found that a Mrs. Norton, long since dead, *had* been a friend of Mr. and Mrs. Nathan Thornes.]

CHAPTER IX

GENERAL REMARKS ON THIS SERIES OF NINE SITTINGS

THE first explanation that occurs to the investigator in these borderland regions is, of course, that of ordinary fraud. The medium is paid for his services—at least, he is when he happens to be a professional, as in this case—and it is to his interest to give good results. Obviously, much detail of genealogical kind may be gleaned by examination of tombstones, and by inquiry. In the sittings under consideration, a large part of the evidence is of this kind; and it is therefore necessary to decide, before going into more perilous hypotheses, whether *all* the knowledge displayed by the medium could or could not be reasonably explained by supposed detective-work, plus an allowance for possible hints dropped, unnoticed, by the sitters, during the proceedings.

If Mr. Watson is an honest man, it is unfortunate for him that his phenomena are so largely of the class (the "tombstone" kind) which specially suggest normal acquisition. In this research, it is necessary to assume that a medium is " a fraud until we have proved him honest "—as the business maxim runs—and I confess that my own attitude towards a new medium is one of curiosity, and a setting of myself to the task of finding out his particular *modus operandi*, rather than one of expectation that anything supernormal will occur. Here perhaps it may be permissible to make a personal remark concerning the sitters. It has often been objected by sceptics—or rather disbelievers, who generally are not " sceptics " in its true meaning—that psychical researchers are mostly professors, literary men, scientific men, and so forth, and that they are easily diddled by a medium, because of their ignorance of mankind, and of the ways of this wicked world generally, outside the walls of libraries and laboratories. Well, in the sittings described in this book, the sitters are probably not open to the charge of any academic innocence and guilelessness. One of the drawbacks of a business life (spiritually speaking) is that it makes a man suspicious of everybody else. His financial existence depends on his acuteness—on his being able to see through the man who is trying to " do " him. And certainly a commercial training inculcates accuracy. I suggest, then, that the sitters mentioned, having been reared in the business atmosphere of large towns, and being in more or less direct connection with business matters (true even of Mr. Oddy), are perhaps rather specially unlikely to be gulled by elementary forms of cheating, and also specially unlikely to accept any "supernormal" hypothesis without being driven to it by sheer weight of otherwise inexplicable facts.

All the sitters now affirm their belief that some such "supernormal" hypothesis is necessary, though at the beginning of the series all except Mr. Knight were disbelievers. The medium never "fishes," never seems to make shots in order to provoke remarks which shall put him on the right track. It is also evident to all who sit with him that he is fond of talking; consequently, the sitters need not say much, and can thus avoid risk of slips. While he is reeling off his evidential statements, he seems to be in a slightly abstracted state—though never approaching trance—and sometimes appears to be listening, or exercising some inner sense which requires the outer ones to be unemployed. I am inclined to think, therefore, that the allowance for hints picked up normally from the sitters—who, moreover, were very careful—may safely be put at almost *nil*.

Now as to tombstones and inquiry. It is just possible that the genealogical details concerning F. K. and I. O. might be obtainable by research. But the research would not be an easy one. The burial-places of some of the deceased people concerned are 100 miles from the town of the sittings, and another town where a cemetery would have to be visited is 40 miles away in the opposite direction, while yet another is 30 miles away, again in a different direction. The railway fares would be a rather serious matter. Here it may be mentioned that the medium's fees are not high. I think five shillings per sitting was the amount usually paid by F. K., but I have known this medium refuse payment altogether, after a poor sitting. In my case, for instance, he at first declined payment, but finally accepted half-a-crown, out of which he had to pay a railway fare of eightpence. If he is a fraud, it is clear that his great powers of deception are coupled with a very unusual lack of acquisitiveness on the financial side.

But, waiving this point, are there any features in the sittings, which are absolutely *inexplicable* by any supposition of detective-work, and which therefore, if chance coincidence also is unacceptable, supply *proof* of "supernormality"?

There are, I think, several that are fairly evidential. For example, the Stonor incident, concerning financial help given by F. K.'s mother—a fact known to no more than two or three living people, so far as can be ascertained; the incident of Mrs. H. K.'s eyes; the correct facts about Kenneth Mills, and about the relatives of Miss Renton, who appeared unexpectedly at a sitting, who lives at a considerable distance (30 miles) and whose ancestors lived at a much greater distance. If we suppose that the medium had been hunting up tombstones, we must allow that he would not have much profit left out of his fees. But, even granting that he does not seek profit, how did he learn about the Stonor affair,[1] and the carefully kept secret of the contemplated extension of business by Mr. Knight's firm,[2] and the state of his sister-in-law's eyes,[3] and his own domestic worries[4]? And, finally, what about the "seven minutes to eight" incident, which seems to me perhaps the best in the whole series? Perhaps it may be suggested that a servant heard F. K. make his request, and repeated it to the medium. We cannot disprove such an assumption, but we can point out that there is no basis for it in actual fact. F. K.'s servants were not spiritualists,

[1] Sitting 7. [2] Sitting 4. [3] Sitting 6. [4] Sitting 7.

they were unknown to the medium except as seeing him come to the house (so far as can be ascertained), and, finally, F. K. has no reason to suppose that any one *did* overhear him. And it is hardly likely that he would unconsciously give the case away by telling the medium about it, retaining no recollection of his slip. This incident, it seems to me, is strongly evidential of some form of supernormal faculty on the part of the medium. And, adding to it the correct statements given to new and unexpected sitters, and the multitudinous facts which a normal memory would find it very difficult to keep in proper order (*e. g.*, nearly thirty family names, with many descriptions, dates, etc.), it will seem, I think, even to an outsider, unlikely that common fraud is an adequate explanation of the phenomena.

If, then, fraud is dismissed as inadequate or improbable, the next explanation to which we turn is that of telepathy or thought-transference; though, in this kind of phenomena, a better name would be "mind-reading." For the active principle concerned, if it is an incarnate mind, is certainly the mind of the medium. The sitters were not usually trying to "telepath" anything; they were mainly occupied in observing and noting. And, in several instances, veridical details were given which were not consciously known to any of the sitters—such as the Christian name of Geoge Stonor. In this case the explainer by mind-reading will have to assume that F. K. had once known the name, and that it was still accessible (though slipped down below the "threshold") to the foraging mind of the medium. It may be so. But it is no more than assumption.

It is of course quite clear—and F. K., I. O., and myself wish to emphasize the fact—that some of the details given are to be explained on mind-reading or clairvoyant lines, if supernormal agency is admitted at all. For example, the vision of Mr. and Mrs. Herbert Knight. It is possible that the medium's keener hearing—we may grant possible hyperæsthesia—may have enabled him to become aware, consciously or subconsciously, of H. K.'s entry, though it was unperceived by the sitters. But no hyperæsthesia will account for the veridical detail of Mrs. H. K.'s inflamed eyes. This seems to demand some kind of clairvoyance, or at least a reading of H. K.'s mind. Also, many of the facts concerning the health of sitters or their relatives, and other details, seem to be attributable to a direct reading or "sensing," by supernormal means, of the conditions in question.

If, then, *some* of the phenomena may be thus explained, the question arises as to whether *all* are not explicable on the same hypothesis. Most of the veridical details given were known consciously, or may be assumed to have been known subconsciously, to some one or other of the sitters. Does the medium's "subliminal," then, forage in the sitters' minds, somehow managing to select the right facts appropriate to the personality who is supposed to be communicating? This, I believe, would be the hypothesis favoured by Mr. Podmore, if he admitted any supernormal agency at all.[1] To me, the idea is unsatisfactory. It is indeed almost ludicrous. Certainly it makes too much demand on my credulity. I confess my utter inability to believe it. There seems, moreover, to be little or no evidence in its support, outside the phenomena which it is invoked to explain. I put aside, then, the hypothesis of selective telepathy as being scientifically unsatisfactory. Let us consider another speculation, which rather attracts me, though I do not fully accept it. A little digression is necessary in order to introduce it.

[1] Mr. Podmore's death, by which psychical research loses a valued worker, occurred after the writing of this chapter.

The form of supernormal function of which I am most strongly convinced, is that which may be called medical diagnosis by a trance-personality. I am forced to the belief, from my own experience, that some trance-controls, on being given a lock of hair or other *rapport*-object, can accurately describe the state of health of an absent person, even though the sitter (the individual bringing the hair) may be quite ignorant of what is the matter with the patient. In other words, the process, whatever it is, is not thought-transference from the sitter. I will give an example.

Mrs. Robinson, an old friend of ours, took a lock of hair which had been cut from the head of an ailing cousin, to a sensitive—well known to me—whose control purports to be a doctor. The cousin lives at a distance of 100 miles from here, and his mother sent the hair by post. The important thing to note is that Mrs. Robinson had not the slightest idea of what was the matter. Her aunt had given no indication whatever as to the nature of the illness. Yet the control diagnosed without hesitation, and Mrs. Robinson took such detailed notes that she covered nine pages of note-paper in her report to the aunt. The lad's illness was an unusual one —an obstruction between nose and throat;

therefore less likely to be hit on by chance coincidence than such common ailments as, *e. g.*, indigestion. Every detail of the diagnosis was correct, and one statement was specially interesting. The control described a slight redness, as of eruption or inflammation, on one side of the patient's face; remarking, however, that it was unconnected with the illness, and was unimportant. Mrs. Robinson was as ignorant concerning this as she was concerning the patient's general health; but, on receiving her aunt's next letter, she found that the description was correct. Her cousin had been suffering from neuralgia, and a mustard leaf had been applied, causing temporary redness and incipient blistering.

Such cases are, naturally, unconvincing to those who do not know the persons concerned; but to me this case is impressive. My knowledge of Mrs. Robinson—who is no novice in these matters, and who is quite alive to the evidential importance of being sure that she knew nothing of the illness—is such that this case of itself would strongly incline me to doubt the universal applicability of telepathy in explanation of such cases. And I have known other cases of equal strength.

I am not, of course, arguing for "spirits"; my point is simply that telepathy from the sitter is an insufficient hypothesis. (It happens to be a fact that in these cases the control usually purports to be a deceased medical man; but I am not concerned with that at present.) Now it sometimes happens that a *rapport*-object is unnecessary. A trance medium well known to me can diagnose without *rapport*-object when the person who sits on the patient's behalf is closely connected with the latter. The sitter seems to supply the necessary link.

Suppose now, that a medium's supernormal powers are directed to the ascertainment of the names and descriptions of a sitter's deceased relatives, instead of to the diagnosis of his living relative's ailments; somewhat as a dowser can "set himself" to find hidden coins as well as underground water. May it not be that a sitter may act as a *rapport*-object or link, enabling some subconscious part of the medium's mind to reach the facts required? And here let me say that the word *rapport* may give a false impression if it suggests a *telepathic* rapport. I have grounds for believing that, in a diagnosis of an absent person's illness by means of hair or other object, the process is *not* telepathic. For one thing, the diagnosing intelligence does not seem able to tell what the owner of the object is doing, at the time of the sitting, as we might reasonably expect if the object coupled up the two minds. Further, the diagnosis, though turning out accurate, sometimes conflicts with the beliefs of the patient and those about him. (Some "telepathists" may suggest that the patient's "subliminal" knew, and that the medium read *that*. We could of course explain almost anything by a supposed reading of a subconsciousness which is supposed to know. It is magnificent—but it is not science.) However, I do not press these points, for I have not sufficient data to feel sure; but I do believe, as a result of much investigation of a medium during many years and with the help of several different sitters, that the *rapport*-object does not bring about a *telepathic* perception. It seems more as if the object carried with it so much of the owner's personality that his whole condition becomes visible, somewhat as a doctor may be able to describe fairly accurately the external appearance (as to complexion and weight) and internal condition of an absent person, after testing and microscopically examining a specimen of his blood, or sputum, or other secretion. If, then, a *rapport*-object can carry with it information of my bodily state, may it not carry with it other information also? If a lock of my hair—or a worn article of clothing, as with another medium who does *not* go into trance, and who has given me good results—can reveal the state of my heart, may it not reveal other things concerning me as well? And this would presumably come about just the same, if the worn article were taken to the medium after my death. I confess that the result of my inquiries into this phase of mediumship has been to lessen the importance, in my eyes, of many of the early Piper sittings at which objects formerly belonging to a deceased person were presented—the importance, I mean, of the results considered as evidence of communication from the dead.

"But," it will be said, "you have just remarked that a *rapport*-object is not always required. What about it *then?*" True; a *rapport*-object can occasionally be dispensed with, *but only when the sitter is in close touch with the patient.* We can dimly see, I think, how a sitter may serve as *rapport*-object. We all of us influence those with whom we are in close contact. They bear the effects of our personality in their minds, and, consequently, in their bodies, brains, etc. May it not be that this impression may be "read off," as the personality-impression may be read off from a lock of hair? Or at least may it not put the medium's subconsciousness "on the track" of other required knowledge? It may seem that this is a far-fetched supposition, for, though it is fairly easy to conceive of a lock of hair yielding information concerning its owner, it is difficult to see how the traces of our personality in other people—even near relatives—can be so distinct; for those traces must be very much mixed up with the traces of other people who also have influenced the sitter. This may be admitted. But at least when the "communicator" purports to be the sitter's father or mother, there is undeniably a close connection. If I had taken some of my mother's hair, during her lifetime, to the mediums I have mentioned, I should probably have received a medical diagnosis of her state of health; if I had taken it after her death, I should probably have received a description of my mother, with details of her last illness, and also with the remark that she was now dead.[1] If I have none of her hair, but if I go myself, I am in one sense taking no *rapport*-object, but in another sense I *am* taking one, and a very intimate one; for some of my body's cells once belonged to my mother in quite as close a way as her

[1] A friend of mine, a doctor, once took a lock of hair from the head of a dead patient. The control at once said, "This is dead," and rebuked the sitter for trying such an experiment.

hair. Does it not seem easy to believe, then, that my body may serve as a *rapport*-object, from which the medium's sixth sense, or whatever we may call it, can read off facts about my mother?

It was believed by Fechner—following and elaborating an ancient notion, *e. g.*, Plato in the *Philebus*—that an Earth-Spirit exists, bearing the same relation to the earth (including all living matter thereon) as our spirits do to our bodies. We are related to this spirit somewhat as our sensations are related to our total mental fabric; each of us is, so to speak, one of the Earth-Spirit's organs of sense-perception. In it, "dead" people exist, as memories exist in our minds. Presumably, then, dead people can be brought into communication with us if we can touch the right chord of association, much as we "remember" things of which something else "reminds" us. A *rapport*-object, or closely-related sitter, may "remind" the World-Soul of the deceased person from whom communication is desired, and evidence of that person's identity may be forthcoming to any extent; for the World-Soul contains all that person's knowledge.[1]

[1] Professor James thought that "some kind of *anima mundi* thinking in all of us" was a "more promising hypothesis than that of a lot of absolutely individual souls." (*Principles of Psychology*, chap. x.)

Fechner himself, though elaborating this spiritual conception of the Universe (for the Earth-Spirit is but a member of a great Ultimate Spirit), nevertheless disliked spiritistic phenomena and notions, though his system could make room for them, if necessary. He did not believe, however, that dead people lost their personalities when they ceased to be the World-Soul's perceptions, and became only its memories; though here there seems to me to be some difficulty.[1]

But this system, though possibly true and certainly ingenious in its analogical reasoning, is a metaphysic of the whole of Nature. As workers at a science, it is preferable for us to keep in close touch with the facts of observation, and not to spread ourselves too much into theories of the All, however un-abstract and "thick" they may be. Moreover, the Fechnerian notion, though helping the imagination in visualizing the

[1] Fechner's *Zend-Avesta*, ii., p. 228, etc., German edition of 1906. A digest is contained in his *Buchlein des Lebens nach dem Tode* (English translation, *On Life after Death*, Open Court Publishing Co.). See James, *Pluralistic Universe*, p. 133 *et seq.* Cf. Arnold's famous lines—

> "The spirit of the world,
> Beholding the absurdity of men—
> Their vaunts, their feats—let a sardonic smile
> For one short moment wander o'er his lips;
> That smile was Heine"

"how" of results obtained by sittings with a medium, does not help us much with spontaneous phenomena where there is no material *rapport*-object, as in Mrs. Napier's "Anthony Grace" incident, Miss Smith's veridical rappings (to be described later), and the host of spontaneous veridical happenings which may be found described in *Proceedings S.P.R.*, vol. x., and elsewhere.

Putting aside, then, the fascinating Fechnerian philosophy as too wide to be very useful to us at present, and putting aside the "selective telepathy" idea as being a dubiously-justified guess, unsupported by evidence, there seems to be nothing left but the spiritistic hypothesis according to which, in evidential cases, the communicators are held to be actually what they claim to be, though often communicating under difficulties which limit their manifestation. It is a legitimate hypothesis, and the facts seem to justify its provisional adoption, though there are many serious difficulties in the way. However, difficulties are to be expected when science explores new realms. The puzzling and baffling details may fall into line later on.

At this point, it is perhaps desirable that I should indicate my sentiment, as well as my belief, regarding this question of personal survival of death, in order that the reader may know how much—if anything—is to be allowed for the "personal equation." When there is a strong desire for survival, as in the case of Myers, it is possible, though not inevitable, that the desire may warp the judgment. With me, however, I think this source of possible error is absent. I have little or no desire of that kind. Continued existence—on the average level of happiness of my earth life—has no attraction for me. I should look forward to an "endless sleep" with equanimity and even with satisfaction, as did Socrates of old; for in deep sleep there is at least no suffering.

It seems to me, therefore, that I am as nearly as possible unprejudiced. My intellectual convictions have not been influenced by emotion. They are at variance, rather than in agreement, with my desires. Mr. G. B. Shaw, with his usual exhilarating vigour of language, tells us that "the way to get at the merits of a case is not to listen to the fool who imagines himself impartial, but to get it argued with reckless bias for and against." (*The Sanity of Art*, p. 4.) Apparently, then, the only sensible people are those who argue, or could argue, with reckless bias, for or against. Well, in psychical research (of which, by the way, Mr. Shaw is *not* speaking) we have had a good many of these sensible people—at least, we have had plenty of "reckless bias for and against"—for and against the alleged phenomena and the various interpretations. Mr. Shaw does not say what is to be done *after* the case has been argued out with sufficiently reckless bias. Perhaps he would admit that at this stage there may be uses for the fool who imagines himself impartial. Anyhow, in whatever category Mr. Shaw might place the present humble writer, the latter maintains, not without some fear and trembling, that so far as honest and thoughtful introspection can tell him, he is almost or quite impartial as to survival. Some fluctuations there may be, according to the mood of the moment; a little desire for life, or a little desire for extinction. But the prevailing condition is neutral.

CHAPTER X

SITTINGS WITH WATSON: SECOND SERIES

In the foregoing chapters I have described the early sittings as fully as possible—except for the omission of a few (evidential) details which might have introduced over-complexity—in order that all incorrect statements should be included, and the reader thus placed in a position to see for himself that, whatever the correct theory may be, chance coincidence cannot account for the phenomena. In sittings that present a large amount of incorrect or dubious matter, it is possible that the few successes may be due to lucky shots. In Watson's case, however, it is not so. The correct statements are so numerous and definite, the incorrect ones are so few, and there is such an absence of "fishing," that an explanation by guess-work and chance coincidence is quite out of the question.

Having demonstrated this by full reports

of the first nine sittings, it seems unnecessary—as it certainly would be tedious—to describe other and later sittings with equally scrupulous inclusiveness. These later sittings yielded further evidential matter, but this matter was at times mixed with things that had already been said. When once the full names, ages, and dates of death, of Mr. Knight's mother, uncles, aunts, etc., had been given, any repetition of these was of course devoid of evidential value. I propose, therefore, to *select*, from four later sittings, such incidents as seem evidential of supernormal faculty, or—in a few cases—as seem curious and interesting enough to be included, though not evidential. The selection, however, *almost* amounts to a full report. The omitted matter is small in quantity; and, if it were included, it would not weaken the evidential weight of the sittings, for the proportion of incorrect statements continued to be so small as to be almost negligible, even if we class as incorrect a few unverifiable descriptions which there is reason to suppose may be true of long-dead relatives.

I have omitted, in order to avoid over-complexity, several evidential statements referring to the relatives and occupations of Mr. Oddy and Mr. Newman.

Sitting 10.

Dec. 11, 1907. *Present, Mr. Frank Knight, Mr. and Mrs. Herbert Knight, and the medium.*

Watson felt that some anniversary was near, but could get no particulars. [Mrs. Knight died Dec. 13, 1905. The medium had already got this, in Sitting No. 4.] He then obtained the following message—purporting to come from Mr. Knight's grandmother :—

> "Your father, whom you will scarcely remember, save by name, often is near you, but probably you cannot realize it. Poor Henry! He did not live long to look after his children. Don't get anxious now, boys, for we will do our best, but it is very strange indeed. Your mother cannot do what she wants, but will endeavour to give you more."

Soon after this, the medium saw, associated with Mrs. H. K., a gentleman 44 years of age, a tall, well-built man, a fluent writer, who had died after a short illness several years ago. (Cf. Sitting 5, Chap. VI., p. 51.) The man appeared to be very anxious to give advice concerning a middle-aged lady still living, a blood-relation of Mrs. Herbert's. This lady was stated to be in a critical state of health, and must remove at once from her present home, to return to the old locality of her own people. Then the following came, in writing :—

"I am your father—Wilfrid. You will know me by that. Your mother must leave Y——, or she will not keep well. That is *final*. You have been good to Mother and poor William—he is better now, but how she silently grieves.

"Bert too was good to him, but all good deeds are stored up and are imperishable."

[Mr. Wilfrid Renton is Mrs. H. K.'s father. He died "several years ago." His widow's health was bad, as stated. William (son) had died April 9, 1907. It is true that "Bert" (Mr. Herbert Knight) had "been good" to him. Cf. Chap. VI.]

The medium again felt the influence of F. K.'s grandmother, and was convinced she had something to say about an anniversary. All the sitters knew that the day was the anniversary (according to the day of the week) of Mrs. Knight's death, and some message to that effect was expected. To their surprise, however, the following writing came:—

"On December 29, you may remember that day. It was always a pleasure to me. I shall never forget when your father died. It must be 27 years since now, if I remember rightly. My thoughts get entangled. When at High Elms. What a long time since. Florence and Kathleen and Kenneth Frederic and your mother and all of us were together. What a change. I cannot say more now. Love to you all. H. F. J."

[Note by F. K.

December 29 is my birthday. My grandmother never forgot it. The last words she ever wrote were words of affectionate greeting to me on my birthday, and are headed "December 29th, 1902."

My father died very suddenly through the breaking of a blood-vessel, and my grandmother had specially felt the shock. She and my mother were the only people in the house, besides my father, when it happened.

The persons mentioned as being "together" did live together "a long time since"—viz., my grandmother, mother, uncle, and two aunts—before marriages, etc., broke the circle. They did not live at High Elms, though that property did belong to the family. They lived about two hundred yards away, and no doubt were often there. I know no one to whom the initials H. F. J. would apply; perhaps they are intended to specify my brother, myself, and my sister—Herbert, Frank, and Janet.]

A little later, Watson got the following writing:—

"Suffer little children to come unto me. Nora Knight was a lamb for his kingdom, but not now as a child do you behold her, but as a maiden fair.

"In Earth-life but briefly. In life immortal for 4½ cycles of time. February to April 1875."

[Mr. Knight's sister Nora was born Feb. 18, 1875, and died April 29 of the same year. F. K. could not recall the dates at the time, and had to look them up.]

Watson also had an impression that Mr. and Mrs. Herbert Knight would not stay long in the house occupied by them at the time. This predicted removal seemed unlikely, but within two months of the sitting they received notice to quit, the landlord having sold the house. This is not particularly evidential, for the coincidence might be accidental. Watson, like Mrs. Thompson's Nelly, is generally wrong in his predictions; he has not given us more than three or four, mostly rather vague, and certainly not very successful as events turned out.

Sitting 11.

Jan. 8, 1908. *Present, F. K., I. O., and medium: later, Mr. and Mrs. H. K. and Miss Renton.*

Nathan Thornes was described as present, and stated, by writing, that he was trying to "stimulate the influence," so that results should be better. F. K. asked for a test message, say, about the business. The following was the reply:—

"Business has no interest with me at all now. I cannot at all give any idea of business life, except that Uriah Martin and I were always chums in that line.

You must not think we will not convey the messages you desire. It is difficult, inasmuch as it is only momentarily we can grasp the position of affairs, that formerly attached themselves to us."

F. K. asked for something about the communicator's earth friends, and "Mrs. Norton, of Stanbury," was given in answer to the request.

[Uriah Martin was Mr. Nathan Thornes's manager. He died many years ago, and Mr. Frank Knight never knew him. F. K. had no conscious knowledge of any Mrs. Norton, but on asking a very old employé, the latter said that he formerly knew a Mr. and Mrs. Norton very well, and that they were friends of Mr. and Mrs. Nathan Thornes. See p. 71.]

Here Mr. and Mrs. H. K. and Miss Renton came in, the two sisters sitting down beside the medium. They were hardly seated before Watson began to write again, producing the following script:—

"These two young ladies are my *nieces*, the daughters of my brother Wilfrid, so I am their aunt, though they would never know me, but they would know their Aunt Tamar Betty, better than me.

"How glad I am to make this known, for William's sake. I cannot give more just now. Your affectionate Aunt, FRANCES JANE."

In answer to inquiries the communicator stated that she died twenty-eight or twenty-nine years ago, aged 19. The medium further wrote :—

"Abraham. Your Grandfather on father's side—Mary. I am her mother, not her *step*-mother—died at Ripley."

An aunt of Mrs. H. K. and Miss Renton, died before they were born, aged 17 or 19. Name, Frances Jane. An aunt named Tamar Betty is still living, and is well known to her nieces. "Abraham" was these latter's paternal grandfather. "Mary" was his first wife. "I am her [Frances Jane's] mother, not her step-mother," is correct. The girls knew their step-grandmother, but had never known their grandmother Mary, the mother of Frances Jane. This latter died at Ripley as stated. Mrs. H. K. and Miss Renton had a brother named William, who died, as mentioned before, on April 9, 1907. (See Sitting 10, p. 93; also Sitting 5, Chap. VI., p. 51.)

CHAPTER XI

SITTINGS WITH WATSON: SECOND SERIES (*continued*)

SITTING 12.

Feb. 7, 1908. *Present, Mr. Frank Knight and medium; later, Mr. Herbert Knight and Mr. Isaac Oddy.*

WATSON had the impression of an old lady, wearing a cap with long strings. He could not see the face clearly, but knew that it was *not* F. K.'s grandmother, whom he had previously seen several times. He then wrote the following:—

"My dear Son,—I am indeed glad to be able to pen you a line. Through the help of my grandmother I am able to do this, my own power not being sufficient. You would not know my mother's mother, but it is her."[1]

[Here Mr. Knight asked for the name.]

"Nora Upton."

[Correct.]

---

[1] In this impressional or automatic writing, there occur several grammatical lapses and constructional peculiarities which are not characteristic of the ostensible communicator. On any theory, the sensitive's mind may be expected to colour the message.

"For 45 years she has been passed away from the Earth." [Correct.]

"How pleasant are the dwelling-places, where love exists, and mine is imperishable. Dear boy, I love you still as much as ever, nay more, and whenever the chance affords I am near to you. Just as your aspiration, just so is my presence."

(Have you been in contact with any of the others lately ?)

"Yes, your Aunt Kathleen."

(Do you all live together still ?)

"No.

"Life truly is good to live for. It is not in the length of days but in the fulness thereof."

(Is there no way by which I can be made to feel your presence when you are near me ?)

"Only by *my* thought being forced upon you. Thought with us is potent and all-powerful."

(Can you remember some incident in your early earth-life, as a test of identity ?)

"I understand partly what you want, but much difficulty obtains in getting it, as it involves some measure of contact with the persons to do so. Your great-grandmother is helping me in this."

(Do you ever visit your other relatives still living on the earth ? Do you visit my sister, for example ?)

"Yes, *often*."

(In that case, can you give me any description of her home ?)

"No."

(Can you see my home now ?)

"No."

(Can you see *me* physically ?)

"No."

(Will you try to tell me something now which happened—say—during your early married life, which I could not have heard of ?)

"My dear child, could I fix my thought into expression I readily would, but your father and I were so long separated it makes it difficult for me."

(Are father and yourself still together ?)

"Oh, yes." [Pause.] "All our time is in use, for

there is no time limit, and could you at all comprehend the nature of our life, you would soon understand how well we are all occupied. Your aunt Florence Bessie for instance is quite away from us, engaged in work of a delightful nature, but we can, by our thought, closely mingle together."

[Tests again asked for.]

"Could you remember Uncle Benjamin running away from home?"

(How old was he when he did this?)

"About 22 I think."

(Was he away long?)

"No."

(You are quite sure about this matter?)

"He did run away from home. Was away all night. Your Grandmother Thornes was in a terrible fix."

(Do you think any one now living will remember this?)

"I think Kenneth Frederic's wife will. When I left Z—— I was bad."

(Ill?)

"Yes. *You* will not remember."

(Where did you live in Z——?)

"Uppertown."

(Correct, but tell me the name of the house.)

[Pause.]

(Cannot you remember it?)

"Yes."

(Well, tell it me, please.)

"Gone." [Pause.] ". . . I shall have to cease, at least for a while. Give my tenderest love to *all*. . . . There is no love like a mother's, so lasting, deep and true. Your own mother."

[F. K. then asked for the name by which she was known to her intimates. "Kathie" was written. F. K. asked if she was sure: the word was then crossed out, and "Kathie is wrong" was written. The name required is *not* Kathie.]

After a few minutes, the writing recommenced:—

"Dear friend. The personality of this subject is hardly suitable for your Mother's full influence to control it in its entirety. It would be stronger manifested through a female organism."

(Do you know my friends on the other side ?)

" I only feel their presence. I am not closely allied to them. I always took a deep interest in the school."

(What school ?)

" Your school."

(Will you give me your name, please ?)

" No, not at present."

(Will you give me your school number ?)

" I had no number."

(Were you a boy at the school ?)

" No."

(Were you a school official ?)

" No."

(Why are you here ?)

" By law of attraction from the school where you was (*sic*) trained."

(When did you die ?)

" Not dead."

(Are you alive, then ?)

" Yes."

At this point the medium said he felt sure something was wrong. He thought there was some impersonation going on; felt sure the writer was a man, but could get no name. He therefore decided to discontinue.

After a short interval, he stated that he heard the name " William Brown," and asked F. K. if the name was known to him. As a matter of fact, William Brown was the husband of Florence Bessie Brown (*née* Thornes). After his wife's death, he emigrated—about 1877—to New Zealand, where he lived until his death in 1903. F. K. never knew him personally.

The medium further stated, to Mr. Oddy, that a near relative of his had died with painful suddenness [true of Mr. Oddy's mother] and that another relative, living in a neighbouring town (name given), was in some business connected with colours or drugs. [Correct, of a living uncle. The business is dyeing.] Watson then gave the correct initials of this man, but could get no name. "He is no longer a young man. Though externally looking well he is really in a very unsatisfactory state of health, and will require to take very great care of himself." [This also is true. His health lately has not been good.]

[Notes by F. K.

The three photographs which I have of my great-grandmother Nora Upton, show her wearing a cap with strings, as described. The medium had not seen these photographs, of course. (Mr. Knight does not lay stress on this as evidence, but merely as being "noteworthy." Probably most old ladies of that date wore caps with strings. My grandmothers did. J. A. H.)

The name of my Aunt Florence Bessie is given correctly, and for the first time in full. Previously, it had been given as Florence B. Thornes.

The incident relating to my Uncle Benjamin

is possible, perhaps probable, but is unverifiable. "Kenneth Frederic's wife" did not come into the family until ten years later, and does not remember hearing of such an occurrence. I have written to my New Zealand cousins, but no verification seems now obtainable.

"When I left Z—— I was bad. *You* will not remember." I was away at boarding-school at the time, but my sister informs me that mother certainly was ill at the time.

The "impersonation incident"—if such it was—is curious and inexplicable. I do happen to take a deep interest in my old school, and the medium is probably aware that I have been closely associated with the Old Boys' Association, etc. But if it was deliberate and fraudulent, it is curious that he did not supply a relevant name, of some person living or dead, which he certainly could have done without difficulty. The same difficulty arises, on the "telepathic" hypothesis.]

Sitting 13.

March 19, 1908. *Present, F. K. and medium; later, Mr. Herbert Knight, Mr. I. Oddy, and Mr. Newman.*

After a little veridical but not strongly-evidential matter relating to Mrs. Knight's last illness, the medium wrote:—

"My dear nephew. It is gratifying indeed to speak to you, if it can only be done by this means.

"Your mother is truly happy in being able to realize your presence.

"I have become master of the material now, and can reach you by means your mother at present may fail in. Our love is as strong as ever. Your Aunt Kathleen."

At this point, F. K. asked the communicator to mention some of her friends known to him, as evidence of identity. "Mary" was written. ("Mary" is a very common name.) "Polly." (Is that right ?) "Polly—Pollitt. It is your Aunt Kathleen who dictates this to you. She passed from earth-life 32 years ago or thereabouts. 1876." (Are you sure of this ?)[1]

"That is what is imparted. She is trying to catch your desire, and to meet it if possible."

(Then ask her, please, to give the name of some friend—not a relative—as a test.)

"Mary."

(What was this lady's other name ?)

"Polly."

(What was her surname, I mean ?)

"Tranter."

(Where did she die ?)

"High—— Queen's Park. Near to here."

(How old was she ?)

[1] The name of Pollitt was unknown to Mr. Knight, but on mentioning it some time afterwards to his sister, the latter said that "when she was a girl she used to go with Grandmother to see a Miss Pollitt, whose mother was an old friend" [of Mrs. Nathan Thornes].

"Twenty-seven."

(How long has she been dead ?)

"Over 30 years."

(Did I ever know her ?)

"No. Your mother knew her well. I cannot help you more in this way now. Your influence is at present unequal in giving us the power."

(Try to think of some other test, please.)

"I am acting in the capacity of dictator, and can only give you in fragments."

The writing began to tail off, and no further evidential matter was produced. The medium then took articles—watch, etc.—from several of the sitters, for "psychometry." A good deal of miscellaneous veridical matter was obtained, which I omit as being confusing to the reader, and not very important. It was of the familiar type; *e. g.*, Mr. Newman was told that he had recently been engaged in laborious mental work, and that he had lately promised something that would entail rather heavy responsibility. (Mr. Newman had been working for an examination, and had recently become engaged to be married.)

Mr. Knight made inquiries, and found that a person named Mary Tranter did live and die at High Elms, Queen's Park. She died twenty years or more before the date of these sittings.

It is impossible to discover whether she was a friend of F. K.'s aunt, or not; but their respective homes were near, and separated only by fields, so it is at least probable that they were acquainted. In fact, it is likely that they played together as children, about forty years ago.

This is a good example of the difficulty of getting conclusive evidence, in this department. If the statements made concern recent events or matter of wide-spread knowledge, the medium may have acquired the facts normally, and may reproduce them automatically, even if he is quite honest; and if the statements concern events long past, they are apt to be unverifiable. But the Mrs. Norton and the Mary Tranter incidents are certainly rather impressive, if fraud is excluded. And, as already indicated, we are of opinion that many of the phenomena exhibited by Watson are not satisfactorily explicable without the supposition of *some* form of supernormal faculty.

It is perhaps desirable to state here, that Watson himself regards the results obtained for Mr. Knight and Mr. Oddy as quite exceptional in their range and detail. He told me that he has often sat for hours with some sitters, without getting a single "impression" of any kind. Success or failure seems to depend on conditions which are not yet in the least understood, unless indeed we provisionally adopt a spiritistic interpretation, for there certainly seems to be more likelihood of a sitter obtaining good evidence, if he has some beloved relative or friend recently passed to "the other side." Mr. Myers found this to be the case with the sitters whom he introduced to Mrs. Thompson.

Whether this be the reason or not, Mr. Knight seems to make a particularly good sitter. If the sceptic suggests that "good" sitters are those who get excited and in conversation give away the details of their family affairs, I emphatically deny the applicability of any such suggestion either to Mr. Knight or Mr. Oddy. Further, Watson's manner, both normally and when obtaining evidence, is quiet and unemotional, and the atmosphere of the sittings is very ordinary and undisturbed. Finally, there being generally several sitters present, there was every opportunity for watching each other; and it will hardly be maintained that details about Mr. Knight's great-grandmother would be likely to cause great excitement in the minds, say, of Mr. Oddy and Mr. Newman. However that may be, the fact remains that no sitter, throughout the whole series, ever detected any hints being dropped which could have assisted the medium. At some of the sittings, the latter was talking or writing practically the whole of the time, and the sitters were merely listening and note-taking.

At the end of the series just dealt with—there was one more sitting which produced little new matter and which I have therefore omitted—Watson said that he felt he was losing touch with Mr. Knight's connections, and would prefer to discontinue the sittings, at least for a time. The suggestion was adopted. Since then, only one or two further sittings have been held, and not much new matter was obtained, though some of it was rather impressive in its evidential quality. For example, the Mrs. Nathan Thornes communicator mentioned, in reply to a question, certain articles manufactured by the firm of which her husband (F. K.'s grandfather) was head. These articles *were* manufactured by the firm in those days, but the trade in them is long since dead, and the business is now concerned with quite different things.

I do not quote the details, as the narrative is already full enough to give a good idea of the evidence. Moreover, the notes taken at these later sittings were less full than in the former ones, chiefly because of repetitions which now had no evidential importance, and which, consequently, were more or less disregarded.

CHAPTER XII

ANOTHER SITTING WITH WATSON

THE records of this sitting are hardly worth quoting, if their intrinsic value only is considered; for the amount of evidential matter was small, and none of it was impossible of acquisition by "detective work." Consequently, if it stood by itself, it would have no evidential weight; but, having become convinced of the medium's possession of genuine psychic powers, I incline to think that my own results with him were due to them rather than to a fraudulent palming-off of normally-acquired knowledge. What I wish to make clear, is, that I do not put forward this sitting as possessing any evidential value if taken by itself; the more so, as I find it desirable to suppress part of the evidence, lest it should cause pain. In the case of my friends, the concealment of their true names has rendered it possible to quote more fully than would have been feasible if their identities had been disclosed.

Sitting of Aug. 8, 1907. *Present, myself and medium all the time; my sister part of the time.*

After preliminary conversation—in which

of course we were careful to say nothing about our relatives, either living or dead—I asked the medium if he could get anything in the way of psychic evidence. He picked up a book from the table, and began running the leaves through his fingers, without speaking. He did not seem to be reading—indeed, his sight is too bad—but, rather, abstracting his mind, ungearing himself, so to speak, from his surroundings and from his thoughts on the subject we had been talking about. Suddenly he looked up, gazing apparently at a point a little above my right shoulder, and fired off the following, almost more rapidly than I could take it down in shorthand :—

"There is a spirit lady with you. Died at the age of 54. Been dead 21 years. Medium sized. Placid. Bright eyes. Slight colour in cheeks. Neat hair, wavy. Name Mary. Interested in your welfare; been with you since passing away. Was business-like and shrewd—a good manager. Has helped you during your illness."

I did not speak while this was being reeled off, and I do not think anything could have been gathered from my face, for I was bending over my writing (sheet of paper on a book held on my knee) and was more intent on getting it all down *verbatim* than on noticing how far it was correct. My sister was sitting partly behind the medium, and he could not see her face. She did not speak.

When he stopped, I told him that what he

had said applied correctly to my mother, except that, as we remember her, she had no colour—*i. e.*, was always very pale.

After a reference to my health, in which his impressions coincided with the doctor's views regarding the condition—a rare one—of my heart, the medium continued :—

"You have not lived here long. You were not here when your mother died. She indicates unfamiliarity with this house." [Correct.]

He then went on to give the correct name of a living relative of mine, stating that the person in question was still "in the body"; also the correct name of another relative (deceased) with age at death, date of that event, and other evidential matter. This spirit he saw in the room, as he had seen my mother. His description was not quite accurate in one of the details, and moreover was not very specific. But the name, age and date of death were correct.

The medium then turned to my sister :—

"You had trouble nine years ago. Change in your life. [Father died Oct. 1898—*i.e.*, nine years before date of sitting.] You have lived here some little time. [Ten years.] House is saturated with your influence. But you did not come to it new—some one lived here before you. Name 'Corrie' vibrates round me in my mind." [True about the house. "Corrie" unrecognized. A doctor of that name lived near, many years ago, but before this house was built.]

Watson then asked for paper, and tried for

automatic writing. Presently he wrote a word or two. I purposely did not get up to see what it was—I was sitting at a little distance from him—lest my manner should help him to make guesses. *He* looked at the writing, and made a remark which I omitted to note down. I think he said, "That is the name of a house, I suppose ——" or something like that. A few more words were written, and then I looked at the production. It was :—

"Round [scrawled in a shaky hand] Roundfield Place
Yes . . .
Mary."

The "Yes" was apparently in answer to the medium's remark : "That is the name of a house, I suppose." It happens that our address was "Roundfield Place" before we came to the house in which we live now. It was while living at Roundfield Place that my mother died, in 1886.

[Comments.

On this sitting alone, I should have assumed probable fraud. The accurately-given names and dates strongly suggest a reading of the tombstone-inscriptions over our vault in a cemetery half a mile away. And the points in which the medium was wrong are precisely those details which would be difficult to get at by inquiry—thus suggesting that he made guesses, or that he had been wrongly informed by some one whose knowledge was imperfect. For example, my mother was pale, and—as we remarked afterwards, though not to the medium—her hair was not wavy. As it was twenty-one years since she died, an accurate description would not be easy to obtain by inquiry.

But, though the facts thus seem to point to fraud, I am inclined to think that this was accidental. The results of Mr. Knight's and Mr. Oddy's sittings have led me to accept the hypothesis of some form of supernormal faculty on the part of Watson, as, on the whole, the most reasonable explanation of the phenomena. And, when once this is accepted, it is as easy to swallow the whole as a part. I mean that it seems rather absurd to assume a *mixture* of fraud and genuineness, assuming, *e. g.*—as some seem to do—that all the normally ascertainable facts *were* normally ascertained, and only the "impossible" ones due to supernormal faculty. There is much to be said in favour of "erring on the safe side," I am aware; but I think that the "mixture" assumption, though certainly on the safe side, is probably more erring than the "unsafer" one would be.

It is worth noting that if Watson had read the tombstone-inscriptions over our vault, he would have got my *father's* name, age, and date of death. Also, a correct description of my father would have been easily obtainable, for his death was fairly recent, and he was extremely well known, locally. Yet not a word concerning him was obtained at the sitting. If, then, the medium obtained any information concerning my father—either from inscriptions or otherwise—he either forgot part of his ammunition, or exercised artistic restraint in order to puzzle me—which is, of course, possible enough, though I agree with Professor James in regarding this supposition with extreme scepticism. It usually pays best for a fraudulent medium to bring out all his goods. I have not much belief in the theory of deliberate artistic restraint. And, if it was forgetfulness, it is curious that it should extend to every detail concerning my father. On the fraud hypothesis, this medium must be granted a marvellously good memory, and it seems unlikely that he would forget *everything* concerning one of the persons whom he had been looking up. Some little detail, surely, might be expected to have been retained.

It ought to be mentioned that, unless Watson did make investigations with fraudulent intent, he is almost certainly ignorant concerning my family, living or dead. He lives at some distance, in another town, and I doubt if he has ever heard any one speak of me, except Mr. Knight and Mr. Oddy. And these two friends of mine were not acquainted with, and know nothing about, any of my deceased relatives. Consequently there could have been no accidental dropping of information on their part. Also, the cemetery mentioned is not a public one, and it is unlikely that Watson had any *casually*-acquired knowledge of the gravestone-inscription.[1]

I intended this sitting to be the first of a lengthy and carefully-planned series, with verbatim notes, and new sitters introduced as often as possible, unexpectedly. Unfortunately, illness prevented me from carrying out this scheme, but I still hope that it may be possible, later on. This medium, however, is not easy to catch, as he is away from home most of his time, giving clairvoyant tests and speaking at meetings in different parts of the country. Also he is only with difficulty persuaded to give private sittings, for he is always afraid he will not be able to "get" anything, and is much distressed and disappointed when this happens.]

[1] It is perhaps just worth saying, though I lay no stress on it, that if my mother could really communicate with us, the words "Roundfield Place" are the most likely words we can think of her saying, as evidence of identity. This had not occurred to us before, but after the sitting we realized how intimately associated with ourselves, in my mother's mind, the words "Roundfield Place" must have been.

CHAPTER XIII

HALLUCINATIONS

It is recorded of a witty Frenchwoman—was it Mme. de Staël?—that she did not believe in ghosts, but she was nevertheless afraid of them. Probably many people are in a similarly illogical state of mind. It seems likely, however, that the next generation will believe more and fear less. Fear is largely due to ignorance of the feared object. "Men fear death," said Bacon, "as children fear to go in the dark." So with Hamlet, in the famous Soliloquy. "For in that sleep of death what dreams may come." But if ghostly phenomena—supposing them to occur—could be understood, there would be good hope that the fear would vanish. The ticking of a watch, held close to the ear, has struck terror into the heart of a savage who could hardly be expected to have any nerves at all. When he understood that it was not some kind of hitherto-unknown and possibly venomous animal, but a useful man-made article, his fears were allayed.

So with ghosts. We are beginning, or think we are beginning, to understand them. The first step in the process was to rechristen them, in order that they might seem more scientifically respectable. Accordingly, they became "visual hallucinations." If apparently connected in some causal way with a distant person, they are "externalizations of a telepathic impact" originating in that person, or this latter perhaps rejoices in a "phantasmogenetic diathesis." Whether these beautiful polysyllables really get us much "forrarder," may be disputed. Naming is not explaining; and some of the terminology is strongly suggestive of the famous *bachelierus* in Molière's *Malade Imaginaire*, who explains that opium produces sleep because it has a "dormitive virtue." Still, psychical research terminology is not quite as bad as that, and, anyhow, if it helps to make the subject respectable—helps to induce orthodox science to regard it as worthy of study—the polysyllables will not have been in vain.

Edmund Gurney neatly defined a hallucination as "a percept which lacks, but which can only by distinct reflection be recognized as lacking, the objective basis which it suggests."[1] An illusion, on the other hand, is a misinterpretation of sensations derived from a real "objective basis," as when an overcoat, hanging in a dim light, is mistaken for a person. It has been objected, not

[1] Cf. James's *Principles of Psychology*, ii., pp. 115, 123, 124.

without grounds, that the term "hallucination" begs the question by assuming that there is nothing really "there," that the experience has no external cause, but is inner, subjective, centrally-initiated, entirely on a par with ordinary dreams, or the delusive visions of a delirious or drugged person. There is some point in the objection; moreover, "hallucination" in ordinary use inevitably suggests mental infirmity, in spite of the hallucinatory experiences of such very sane folks as Socrates, Luther, Napoleon, and Ben Jonson. Still, there seems to be no satisfactory substitute at present. It must therefore be borne in mind that the word as used in psychical research, whatever its popular connotations may be, carries with it no implied suggestion of any morbid condition, and does not prejudge the question as to whether the experience is entirely subjective or not.[1]

Hallucinations may affect any of the senses, but the most important are visual and auditory. These latter are often difficult to establish; for ordinary noises, even though inexplicable, may be caused by rats, water-pipes, or other very matter-of-fact things. But occasionally it seems possible to exclude these agencies. A friend of mine once heard

[1] Mr. Piddington has shown, fairly conclusively, that between psychical and "visceral" hallucinations due to pathological conditions, there is a well-marked generic difference. *Proceedings S.P.R.*, vol. xix., p. 267.

footsteps outside his bedroom door, and went out to investigate. No one was there, but the footsteps were still audible, tramping slowly down the stairs. My friend leaned over the rail, and—so to speak—watched them down. When they reached the bottom, where the stair-carpet ended and linoleum began, the sound changed as it would have done under real feet. It was about four o'clock on a June morning, and, consequently, broad daylight. The footsteps were heard by my friend's wife and by his brother. All are very serious and honest people, but queer things do happen in that house, apparently in connection with the wife, who shows marked psychic faculties, but declines to attempt any development. My friend is a phlegmatic man, of normal mind and great physical strength. He is a determined materialist. Such incidents, however, are not "evidential."[1] The following is a better case.

A few years ago (exact date given me) Miss Smith was staying with her sister in the house of Mrs. Jones, in a tiny northern village. One evening a messenger brought the informa-

[1] Cf. Lang's *Dreams and Ghosts*, p. 189: a "footstep case" in which the seventeenth and eighteenth steps always creaked, as those two steps—and those only—did under real feet. Percipient was a lady well known to Mr. Lang. She sat on the stair and "watched" the footsteps down. But, in this case, there was apparently no other percipient, and the experience might be subjective only.

tion that Miss Smith's brother Tom, whose business was in a town a few miles away, had been hurt; but in his occupation slight accidents are common, and the girls were not alarmed. They retired for the night soon after nine o'clock. Just as the sister was getting into bed, and before Miss Smith had finished undressing, both of them heard a succession of sounds as of heavy blows struck on the wall. The part of the wall on which they occurred was an out-wall—*i. e.*, did not adjoin any other room or building—and the outside of that part could be seen by looking out of the open window; further, the month being June, there was light enough not only to see but also to recognize any human being, or any living thing big enough to cause the sounds. The sisters looked out, and Miss Smith climbed out on a ledge in the roof, in order to have a better view, but nothing was discovered. Meanwhile the knocking continued. Mrs. Jones was fetched, and further investigation made, but without result. Eventually the girls went to bed, though not to sleep; for the knocking continued until three o'clock in the morning, causing great terror. (The fright, and the general tension, brought on in Miss Smith's case an attack of brain fever, though she is one of the calmest and most unemotional women I have ever known.) Early in the morning, a messenger brought the news that Tom Smith had died at 8.45 the previous night—about twenty or twenty-five minutes before the noises began. A curious feature of the sounds was that they were not audible in the other rooms, though in this one room they seemed loud enough to be heard all over the house.

Miss Smith has been well known to me for many years. I cross-examined her closely, and also obtained an independent account from her sister, with the result that it seemed unlikely that the sounds were due to a normal cause. If they were not, the experience was an auditory hallucination; and it seems also to have had a veridical (truth-telling) element, for it coincided with the death of Miss Smith's favourite brother. However, I quote the case chiefly as illustration, for its evidential strength is not very great. Of course, even if we attribute the sounds to the agency of the man's surviving mind, we need not suppose that they were consciously and deliberately produced; for to terrify his favourite sister into brain-fever would be far from his wish. It is probable, as was thought by Myers, that in such cases the agent is not present in anything like the fulness of his personality—is not aware of the effects which he is producing in our world. It may be that these phenomena are the dreams of the dead, or are produced in a dream-like and unreasoning state, such as it is natural to expect would be a spirit's condition after the wrench of death. There is reason to suppose, from the Piper and other phenomena, that some such condition usually does supervene before the spirit comes to itself in the new environment.

Let us pass now to visual hallucinations. First, what are the results which the S.P.R.'s laborious investigations may be said to have established?[1] They seem to me to be as follows.

(1) That a person in good health, of apparently perfect sanity, awake, and in a normal and unexcited frame of mind, may see an apparition of a person whose body is elsewhere. The apparition may be that of a living or a dead person, who may or may not be known to the percipient.

(2) That though some of these apparitions are merely subjective hallucinations similar to those which may be produced hypnotically or which arise through bodily abnormality due to disease or drugs, there is nevertheless reason to believe that many of them are something more. The chief reasons —to be dealt with later—for so believing, are (*a*) that an apparition is sometimes seen by more than one person, (*b*) that in many cases there seems to be a connection between

[1] These investigations were carried out by means of inquiry among nearly 20,000 people. It was a "Census of Hallucinations." *Proceedings*, vol. x.

the fact of the apparition and some other fact concerning the real individual whose "ghost" appears—*e. g.*, in many cases, that individual is found to have been going through some unusually stressful experience (as dying) or, perhaps, as in some carefully-recorded cases, trying to produce an apparition of himself to the percipient, merely as an experiment.

The explanation of these phenomena, the reality of which is admitted by all investigators, is a difficult matter; but there seems little doubt that the safe starting-point must, at least for the present, be the idea of thought-transference or telepathy. The experiments recorded in the *Proceedings* and *Journal* of the Society for Psychical Research are sufficient, I think, to convince a logical and unprejudiced reader that thought-transference between two minds is possible; that by concentration and willing, the agent has somehow caused the desired idea, as of a triangle or other figure or object, to arise in the percipient's mind, without any indication being perceived through the ordinary sensory channels.[1] Close proximity is not a necessity, for experiments have succeeded when agent and percipient have been at a distance of several miles from each other.[2] In most of

[1] See also Sir Oliver Lodge's *Survival of Man*, p. 38 and foll.

[2] *Journal S.P.R.*, vol. xii., p. 223. Distance 20 miles.

these cases the percipient does not see the object externally, but rather perceives it by an inner vision; or the idea may merely "arise," as many ordinary ideas do, without apparent cause. But in many instances the object presents itself to a good visualizer as externalized in space—*i. e.*, as a definite hallucination.[1] Of this kind are those remarkable cases [2] in which the agent has succeeded in making the percipient see an apparition of himself; the percipient, be it noted, having no knowledge of what was being attempted, and therefore in no state of expectancy.

We thus arrive, by gradual approach from simple cases of thought-transference, at a point from which apparitions may be explained on the same principle. A living person can affect another mind by means other than the known methods of communication, even to the extent of producing his own "ghost"; if, then, the apparition of a dead person is seen, is it not possible to suppose that the personality of that individual is still somehow existent, and trying to make itself manifest? On the face of it, it seems reasonable; but several objections require to be considered.

One difficulty is that whereas the living

[1] Dr. Gibotteau's case. *Proceedings S.P.R.*, vol. viii., p. 466.

[2] Myers's *Human Personality*, vol. i., pp. 293, 688, 690, 692. In one case the distance between agent and percipient (Mr. S. H. B. and Miss Verity) was three miles.

experimenter has a material brain, which may do the trick by starting some sort of "waves," the supposed dead experimenter has not. This difficulty of course depends on the assumption that mental activity cannot take place without a material brain, of which thought is a "function." A discussion of the materialistic position would be out of place in this book; for present purposes it suffices to point out that the materialist's assumption—that in all the Universe no intelligence exists apart from what we call nervous systems—is a tremendous assumption to make. It is surely rather rash to make such arbitrary decisions as to what is or is not possible in a universe which, as we learn more about it, is ever becoming more wonderful and more complex. And if the materialist disclaims dogmatism and says that he merely "sees no reason" to suppose discarnate Intelligence—no evidence for its existence—the reply is that if he will read the publications of the S.P.R., he will probably never again say that there is *no evidence* for the existence of such intelligence, though it is quite open to him to say that it is not sufficient to convince him.[1] Further, there is some ground, in the nature of the evidence, for the supposition that telepathy is not a

[1] None are so blind as those who will not see. I know a worthy cleric who "can see no evidence for evolution."

physical process. In many cases, the agent has been asleep, and the brain-activity therefore probably at its lowest ebb.[1] Also, the complexity of the apparition is often such as to render it difficult to believe that it is an affair of ether-waves or other physical means of transmission. And if the process is superphysical (as Mr. Gerald Balfour, among others, believes), a physical brain is not a necessity.

So much for the argument of the materialist. There are, however, other and perhaps more weighty objections to the belief that an apparition of a dead person is generated by that person's surviving mind:—

(1) The apparition may be a merely *subjective* hallucination. This is no doubt true in many cases, but the supposition is less acceptable when several people see the ghost,[2] or when the percipient had made a "compact" with the person whose ghost appears, but whose death had not become known to the percipient at the time of the vision.[3] It is also unlikely that a vision is entirely subjective when the percipient, while not recognizing the apparition—it being that of an unknown person—is able to describe it so that it is

[1] This was so in some of the experimental cases already alluded to—*e.g.*, that of Mr. Godfrey, *Human Personality*, vol. i., p. 688. Cf. also Mr. Newnham's case, *ibid.*, p. 418.

[2] *Human Personality*, vol. ii., p. 389.

[3] Case of Countess Kapnist, *ibid.*, ii., p. 49. Other cases, p. 42.

recognized by people who knew the deceased,[1] or picks the correct photograph out of a number.[2] As to those cases in which the person dies about the time at which his apparition is seen (by people unaware of his death) it is obvious that this may sometimes be a chance coincidence; the percipient may happen to have a subjective hallucination just at the right time. But it was shown by the results of the Census of Hallucinations that the actual coincidences are much more numerous than chance would require. Chance would bring about a coincidence of the kind in one out of 19,000 cases of apparition; the *actual* proportion for this number was found to be 440.[3] This does not prove anything absolutely, for there is great difficulty in estimating the proper allowance for possible error—lapse of memory and other sources of inaccuracy. But it is at least a striking fact, and the committee dealing with the Census seem to have been liberal in their discounting for all possible sources of error.[4]

[1] Case of Mrs. Bacchus. *Human Personality*, ii., p. 34. In this case, as often, there was a special reason for this spirit appearing in this particular house. The widow of the man whose apparition was seen, had died in the house the night before, and the body was lying in the room below. I suppose Dr. R. had come "to meet his wife."

[2] *Spirit Teachings* (Stainton Moses), p. xix.

[3] See *Proceedings*, vol. x., for full particulars, and for the mathematics of the subject, p. 247.

[4] The Committee comprised Prof. and Mrs. Sidgwick,

(2) An apparition may be a telepathically generated phantasm, the agent being some living person. If a living agent can project his own *eidolon*, perhaps he could produce an *eidolon* of somebody else. This, though a rather far-fetched idea, and at present unsupported by much evidence, is nevertheless a legitimate hypothesis. It seems, however, an improbable one in "compact" cases, when the compact to "appear" is known to very few people, and the probability therefore being that no person possessing the apparently rare phantasmogenetic faculty will happen to be among that number. And the likelihood that a living person has "telepathed" the apparition seems sometimes to be negatived by specific features in the phantasm which were known to one living person only.[1] It would, of course, be more

Miss Johnson, Mr. Myers, Dr. Myers, and Mr. Podmore Their conclusion was that "between deaths and apparitions of the dying person a connection exists which is not due to chance." *Proc.*, vol. x., p. 394.

[1] Case of Mr. F. G. *Human Personality*, ii., p. 27. The deceased girl had a scratch on her face, accidentally caused by the mother after death. No one but the mother knew of this. But the scratch was visible in the apparition, seen by a brother nine years after death. On the telepathic hypothesis, the mother was the agent; but we have no reason to suppose that she possessed such powers. (This case cannot be explained by the theory of an emergence of a latent telepathic message sent by the "agent" before death; for the apparition conveyed information which was not known to the sister while living.)

satisfactory if we could get a well-authenticated case in which the apparition revealed a verifiable fact which was known to no one left on earth; but this would only happen by a very fortunate concatenation of circumstances, for most facts of this kind would be unverifiable—and, anyhow, clairvoyance and latent telepathy would have to be reckoned with, so the case would not be crucial. There is, however, some evidence for messages of this kind, though not hallucinatorily given;[1] and this supports by analogy the *primâ facie* explanation of many apparitions, as against an explanation by telepathy from the living.

On the whole, then, it seems reasonable to suppose that the cause of an apparition of a dead person *may* be the surviving mind of the person who appears; though, as already remarked in connection with the auditory experience of Miss Smith, it is not necessary to believe that the full personality of the deceased is concerned. In the experimental cases of Mr. Kirk and Mr. S. H. B. (who happens to be the brother of a friend of mine) the agent did not know whether or not he had succeeded in "appearing," until he heard the percipient's story; similarly, a disembodied person trying to appear, may not know whether he is succeeding or not. Further, the phantasm of a living person sometimes appears, *without*

[1] *Human Personality*, vol. ii., pp. 37, 183.

that person's conscious will or effort, though in veridical circumstances which suggest that his mind must be concerned, evidently in its subliminal levels. This further supports the conjecture that an apparition of a dead person, even though in some way proceeding from that person's mind, is not necessarily the manifestation of full consciousness. This view is strengthened by the aimless and semi-conscious behaviour of many veridical apparitions, and would seem to be necessitated by some cases of haunting. Apparitions, then, may be—in Myers's striking phrase—the objectified dreams of the dead. But, if they can dream, they are not very dead.[1]

So far of spontaneous apparitions among ordinary folks. What now of the forms seen by the medium Watson ? May not these have an external cause, like the spontaneous ones ?

[1] Mr. Lang has remarked that the theory, in origin, is due to St. Augustine, and that Thomas Aquinas held a similar opinion. (*Cock Lane and Common Sense*, pp. 132–3, 156; also *Book of Dreams and Ghosts*, p. 16, giving quotation from *De Cura pro Mortuis Habenda*, Library of the Fathers, *XVII. Short Treatises*, pp. 530–531.) But it is probably almost as old as the earliest theories on the subject. As to the Church Fathers, they were apt to believe, like the good Sir Thomas Browne of a later date, that " apparitions and ghosts of departed persons are not the wandering souls of men, but the unquiet walks of devils." (*Religio Medici*, xxxvii.) The departed, being in Hell, Purgatory, or Paradise, could not " appear." This is still the Roman Catholic attitude, as exemplified by Father Hugh Benson and Mr. Raupert.

The dreams-of-the-dead notion, though a plausible explanation of some cases of a spontaneous kind, seems quite out of it here. If the dead are the agents at all, they are very wide awake; for the evidence of identity is presented with undeniable intelligence. It is possible, however, to avoid invoking their agency, if we assume that the medium obtains, telepathically or clairvoyantly, some knowledge of the dead people concerned, and that this knowledge objectifies itself; much as if, in the case of a dowser, a hallucination of running water, veridical as to quantity and direction, were experienced when over hidden water-pipes. Some of the incidents are of this character—*e. g.*, Mrs. H. K.'s veridical apparition in Sitting 6, Chap. VI., p. 56. Another curious affair—a sensing without hallucination—occurred at a sitting on Dec. 11, 1907, when Watson complained of the "perturbed conditions." He said he thought that a somewhat excited discussion had recently taken place in the room, and that the psychical vibrations thus set up were not yet dispersed. Consequently he had difficulty in getting impressions, as "the spirits could not break through this disturbed area without much trouble." As a matter of fact, there *had* been a rather lively though good-humoured argument in that room, a few days before, between Mr. Knight and a friend. There was no reason to suppose that Watson had any normal knowledge of this. On changing to another room, the conditions became better, and the sitting proceeded satisfactorily.

But no such sensing of the immediate surroundings could account for such incidents as those of the Christian names of George Stonor and Mary Hanby; and another curious episode, which I will describe in a few words, tells rather strongly in favour of the deliberate, fully-conscious agency of one of the *soi-disant* communicators.

At a sitting on Feb. 7, 1908, Watson said that Mrs. Knight (F. K.'s mother) was in the room, wearing a handsome brown silk dress, high in the neck, trimmed with white, and having a "lined" or "watered" effect in its texture. There was some history attached to this dress, about which F. K. was to inquire of his sister, who would probably know.

F. K. knew nothing about this, and therefore wrote to his sister, as instructed. The reply was to the effect that Mrs. Knight had ordered a dress such as the one described, but that it was delivered only the day before she died, and, consequently, was never worn. Mr. Knight's sister was able, further, to send a few inches of the brown watered material, with some of the white lace trimming. Both of these I have seen. Watson's description, as far as it goes, certainly applies.

If fraud is dismissed, this incident suggests neither telepathy nor a rummaging among passive memories in a cosmic reservoir; but, rather, the activity of a surviving mind, able to marshal its earth memories and to select from them for presentation to the medium, such details as will constitute the strongest possible evidence of identity.

Leaving now the question of "evidence," a word or two is perhaps required as to the *nature* of visual hallucinations. When these forms are seen, either by mediums like Watson or by ordinary people who have an occasional spontaneous experience of the kind, is there really anything there, in a physical sense? The answer is that we don't know. In Watson's case, I am inclined to think that he does not really see anything with his eyes, though I am not sure. The people are externalized clearly enough to him, and he will describe a "well-dressed man standing on the hearth-rug," or an old lady sitting in the rocking-chair, in the most prosaic manner imaginable. A rather curious thing is that he says he can form an idea as to how long they have been dead, by observing the degree of their apparent materiality. A recently-deceased person looks solid and life-like; an individual long dead (*e. g.*, Mr. Knight's great-grandmother, Nora Upton) is tenuous and shadowy. Perhaps the spirit, as it progresses, travels farther and farther away from material conditions, and becomes less able to produce effects in our world, either on the brain of the medium or on external matter.

Watson himself is sure that he sees the figures, and says he cannot see them with his eyes shut. But this may be due to self-suggestion. It seems more likely that the perception is inner. In the first place, his sight is extremely bad. He has undergone several operations on both eyes, and he has to wear enormously convex glasses. Even with these, he is unable to read. For this purpose he has to reinforce his spectacles with a large lens. Yet in spite of this ocular deficiency he describes these "spirit forms" with extreme minuteness—not only their features and dress, but, often, small articles of jewellery. It seems doubtful if he could do this with living people, in a normal way. Again, when describing the figure of my mother, although his eyes seemed to be fixed on a point above my right shoulder, he gave the impression of being occupied in listening rather than in seeing—as one often stares fixedly, without seeing anything, when thinking abstractedly. Moreover, when he said of another figure (to the other sitter) "she has gone behind your chair," he indicated the alleged movement by a turn of the head, but did not seem to follow a moving object with his eyes. Perhaps, then, in his case the forms are interiorly perceived and are in no sense physically present. But this is no more than a provisional supposition. It is too early to come to any conclusion in the matter. I confess (though the confession is terribly heretical, scientifically speaking) that I see no reason to *deny* that there may be something really " there." By means of our muscles, we move things about. Perhaps we can produce visible effects at a distance of a few inches (in a dry enough climate) by rubbing feet on floor, and presenting a finger at the gas issuing from a burner, thereby lighting it. But, generally speaking, we produce physical phenomena only by pushing or pulling with our muscles. When we come to think of it, however, there seems to be no reason why this limitation should be absolute. It is a matter of habit. We have got accustomed to it, and are apt to accept it as a necessary result of things being as they are. But there is nothing essentially outrageous or absurd in the supposition that a human being may move matter without the use of his muscles, as Eusapia Palladino is alleged to do. " How could it be done ? " it may be asked. We do not know; but then we do not know how we move matter *with* our muscles. I make an effort of will, and my arm moves;

but I do not in the least understand how my effort of will—a mental fact—has produced an effect in the material world. It is altogether marvellous. Between the physics of the brain and the corresponding facts of consciousness, there is—as Tyndall said—a gulf which has not been bridged. Between the movement of my arm and the volitional effort which "caused" it, I can detect no necessary relation. It is familiar to me, and causes no surprise, because it is habitual; but, rationally speaking, it is no less astonishing than it would be if, by a similar effort of will, I upset a chair in the next room, while sitting peacefully in my own. The phenomenon in each case is, at bottom, incomprehensible.

If, then, there seems no *a priori* reason why we should not be able to act at a distance as well as at close quarters, there seems to be no particular difficulty in supposing an actual effect—ethereal or "metethereal," if not material—produced by a distant or deceased person on the portion of space in which an apparition is seen. And of course the same applies to auditory hallucinations such as that experienced by Miss Smith, the collective character of which strongly suggests some actual external cause of a physical or quasi-physical nature. If "spirit-photography" turns out to be a genuine fact—if, say, the case described in Chapter I. is correctly described and includes no deliberate fraud—a more or less physical theory of many veridical hallucinations will take the place of the externalized-telepathic-impact theory which is fashionable at present. It will have to be recognized that there is something really "there." Moreover, there are cases on record in which the apparition has caused some effect in the material world—an effect remaining after the phantasm's disappearance. As, for instance, when it *moves* something; or, as in the case of the Rev. Dr. Gwynne, puts out the light! (*Phantasms of the Living*, ii., p. 202. Both Dr. and Mrs. Gwynne saw the ghost, which was not recognized. It seemed to be a case of "haunting.") But these are not among the well-established phenomena, and, while leaving the door open—so to speak—for future evidence, it must be said that, at present, there is not much good evidence in support of any considerable material effects which are to be attributed, even hypothetically, to a disembodied mind. If messages ever do come from the "other side"—and I believe they do—there must of course be a connection somewhere; but a very small change in the brain of a sensitive would account for a good deal in the way of communications or apparitions. And, observing the axiom of parsimony, we must not make bigger suppositions than the facts necessitate.

CHAPTER XIV

AUTOMATIC WRITING

LET us turn now to the consideration of the other principal feature displayed at most sittings by Watson—viz., automatic writing.

It is probable that human beings have many powers or faculties which we have not yet discovered. We are continually finding out new potencies, even in the chemically simple and unorganized matter of the external world (*e. g.*, radio-activity), and, this being so, it seems more than likely that such a complex structure as the brain of man will be found to possess many properties which are not yet apparent. This is a reasonable supposition, even looking at the matter from the standpoint of the materialist.

The fact of automatism, or the working of muscles without intervention of ordinary consciousness, is common enough. We do not consciously direct the action of our hearts and lungs; they do it "of themselves," or automatically. Similarly with digestion, which, though we think nothing of it, involves amazingly complex chemical processes, and which, when we come to think of it, seems to require intelligence. Yet it is not the intelligence of the normal consciousness, for we are not aware of the reactions which are taking place within us. We call it, therefore, subliminal consciousness, or subconsciousness.

A kind of mind, then, is manifested, or is inferrible, where it is not at first apparent; a mind which, though closely connected with our well-being, is not a part of our normal consciousness. It is this part of our mentality that controls the involuntary muscles (heart, etc.) and the general organic processes of digestion and the like. It can also take charge of some of the muscles which are "voluntary" —*i.e.*, which are usually moved by the *conscious* will; for it is observable that many actions which at first are the result of conscious thought, gradually come to be performed automatically; as walking, writing, sewing, knitting, etc. Long practice has educated the subconsciousness until it can now take charge of the muscles concerned, leaving the supraliminal consciousness free for more original and higher work. Consequently, we may continue to walk with a friend, even while engaged in discussing Bimetallism or the Hegelian philosophy.

But it is experimentally found that there are forms of automatism in which muscles are moved not only in a mechanical and servant-like sort of way, but also in an *unexpected* and *productive* sort of way. In walking or knitting the legs or fingers move "of themselves," but they repeat the same movements continually, and no initiative is required. But it is found by many people that if they take a pencil in the hand, allowing the latter to rest passively on a sheet of paper, written characters or drawn figures will be produced without conscious will or thought. Sir Francis Galton describes his own case as follows :—

"I have myself had frequent experience of the automatic construction of fantastic figures, through a practice I have somewhat encouraged for the purpose, of allowing my hand to scribble at its own will, while I am giving my best attention to what is being said by others, as at small committees. It is always a surprise to me to see the result whenever I turn my thoughts on what I have been subconsciously doing. I can rarely recollect even a few of the steps by which the drawings were made; they grew piecemeal, with some almost forgotten notice, from time to time, of the sketch as a whole. I can trace no likeness between what I draw and the images that present themselves to me in dreams, and I find that a very trifling accident, such as a chance dot on the paper, may have great influence on the general character of any one of these automatic sketches." [1]

Some of the automatic drawings that I have seen are beautifully executed, with a kind of ornate *bizarrerie* which stamps them as very different from consciously-produced designs. From such drawings as these it is but a small step to writing, for they both are symbols of thought, and both must be the

[1] *Inquiries into Human Faculty*, section on Visionaries, p. 124 of Dent's "Everyman" edition.

product of intelligence, conscious or subconscious. Not many people, however, can write automatically with a free pencil, and resort is consequently had to a little piece of apparatus.

In these days of psychical novels, probably most people know what is meant by "planchette," which began more or less as a drawing-room toy, and is now—also more or less—an implement for serious psychological investigation. If two people place their finger-tips lightly on this little heart-shaped board, it will usually be found that movements result, though the experimenters are not consciously pulling or pushing. The movements may only be sufficient to cause the pencil to make scrawls or zigzags on the paper; but, with good operators, words will be written, words which (often) were not in the conscious mind of the operators. Thus there is a definite *product*—a result, apparently, of *subliminal thinking*. This product is often astonishing in its remoteness from the ordinary thoughts of the planchettists, and is frequently—sad to relate—comic or even downright silly. It usually purports to emanate from a spirit—probably because the planchette-tradition is that spirits are the agents, and because the planchettists have that idea in their minds, even though they may not always believe it.

This planchette-product is often interesting

by its mere *bizarrerie*, which suggests a connection with dreams. Indeed it seems likely that if a sleeper could write while he is dreaming, he would produce something very like the average planchette-script. In each case, it is the subliminal consciousness that is at work—or rather, perhaps, at play.

The proportional number of people who can produce planchette-writing is not definitely settled. Out of a dozen taken at random, there will probably be at least two or three. I myself have no automatic faculty, and cannot make the planchette budge at all; but I can play second fiddle—or, to vary the metaphor, can act as carbon to the active zinc—by associating myself with a friend who has the power. *E. g.*, with my friend Hartley we find that the planchette will usually write something, generally something very trivial. We made a long series of trials some years ago, from the contemporaneous records of which I quote.

Our first "spirit," who wrote her name at the second sitting, after abundant scrawls, was "Minnie Murdoch." Both of us were struck by the curious way in which the second word was written. After M was written, the planchette began again, and wrote MU; then a fresh start, and MUR appeared; and so on to the end. Each time, the letters already traced were written with greater ease, as if the consciousness at work were *learning*. We did not expect this, and W. H., who is undoubtedly the moving power, was unboundedly astonished.[1]

Neither Hartley nor I could claim the honour of Minnie Murdoch's acquaintance, so we asked for further information. In answer to various questions, at this and subsequent sittings, we were told that our fair visitor (we politely assume the fairness) was a spirit, that she died at Balloch in 1896 or 1897 (aged fifty, as she remarked with commendable but surprising frankness), that she was attached in a guardian-angel sort of way to Hartley's wife—who is Scottish, hence perhaps the sympathy—and that she hoped we should have "enough money and a merry Christmas." This worldly-sounding and very unspiritual wish caused us rather a shock; though, on reflection, we agreed that it was rather nice of Minnie, and not inconsistent with the presumable activities of a good-natured Scottish spirit. Another good trait was Minnie's evident fear of being behind time with her good wishes; for, though she was giving us Christmas greetings, we were at the time only in October.

After this, we often had other "spirits,"

[1] I rather fancy that the Minnie and the Mu were only the usual zigzags which planchette often indulges in; but H. read the letters into them. After *Mur*, Murphy or Murdoch was almost inevitable.

among them a John Murray, who said that he died in 1796, but who vigorously denied that King George the Third was reigning at the time. A curious feature was that Minnie Murdoch would not write if my friend Hartley was smoking; but she would go ahead at once when he laid down his pipe or cigar. John Murray, however, did not seem to have any objections.[1]

Now I have not the slightest reason to suppose that these good folks were in the least degree genuine. They were probably dream-creations of my co-planchettist's subliminal consciousness. It is true that he himself, though not a spiritualist, is nevertheless disposed to be friendly to the hypothesis that some external agency is concerned; for he feels sure that he is not moving the planchette, and that the things written do not emanate from his consciousness. I quite believe this is subjectively true. He is not consciously moving the planchette, and the messages do not come from his conscious mind. Nevertheless, I believe he is the agent, though subconsciously, in both the physical and the psychical aspect of the phenomenon.

But let us go on to the next step.

It is sometimes found that the planchette

[1] "John" said he had lived in our own town (Bradford) but declined to commit himself to any address or to any identifying details. Perhaps he realized that I was going to "look him up."

writes correct matter which the automatists say they did not know. For example, a friend of mine (Dr. Thornton, a fellow-member of the S.P.R.) planchetting with his daughter, made the acquaintance of a Thomas Bamer, who said he had been a pikeman and had been killed at Flodden. Dr. Thornton immediately proceeded to make a mean use of the advantage which his superior education gave him over the poor unlettered soldier, by asking questions about historical matters, and thus trying to trip up the unfortunate *revenant* :—

Dr. T. What was the date of the battle ?

T. B. 1640.

[Alas, poor spirit ! But the answer was curious, for both the automatists knew well enough that the correct date was 1513. Another proof that the conscious mind is not the agent.]

Dr. T. Who commanded the English army ?

T. B. Sir Edward Stanley.

This astonished Dr. Thornton still more; for he was expecting " Earl of Surrey " to be written, the Earl being, as he knew, the English general concerned. On looking up, however, he found that Sir Edward Stanley did command a part—the left wing—of the English forces, and that this part is specially mentioned as having been composed largely of pikemen. Of these facts, neither Dr. Thornton nor his daughter had any conscious knowledge.

I suggested that one or both had known the facts, but had forgotten them. Dr. Thornton repeated that he felt sure he had never known about Stanley commanding the left wing at Flodden. But I pointed out that the Stanley in question is mentioned in Scott's *Marmion*—and at greater length in the notes to some editions of Scott's Poems—and that therefore the two planchettists in this case could hardly be credited (or debited ?) with ignorance on the point at issue, even assuming that they were innocent of systematic historical knowledge. Still, waiving this, it is at least interesting to find that the planchette wrote something which neither of the automatists *consciously* knew. In other words, it appears that planchette-writing will sometimes resurrect forgotten things—will reproduce submerged recollections or memories. It has consequently been suggested by some perhaps over-hasty speculative philosophers, that we never really forget anything; that all we have known and forgotten, still exists in the subconscious strata of our minds. This is not provable, and is probably too extreme a view. But it is certain that much "forgotten" matter does thus exist in our subliminal memories, and that it can sometimes be reached and brought forth by these automatic methods. In a recent instructive case, a "Blanche Poynings" communicator gave much historical matter which apparently could not have been gathered without a good deal of research. But it was all found in a forgotten novel, of which "Blanche Poynings" was a subsidiary character (*Journal S.P.R.*, xii., p. 287).

There is also often shown a sportive kind of will. A young lady friend of mine and her sister were operating planchette not long ago, and—after the usual manner of such damsels—were asking for information from the spiritual realms, concerning their matrimonial futures. With reference to the lady best known to me, there was written the name "Albert." This was not recognized as applying to any one eligible or likely:—

Question. What is his trade?

Answer. No trade.

Q. What then?

A. Profession.

Q. What profession?

A. Accountant.

Still no recognition. Further details were asked for, and given, without shedding any light on the matter. Finally, a surname was written, and the whole thing was clear. All the details were true, of this particular man, but had not suggested him, partly because the automatists knew him but slightly, and partly because, being already married, he was not in their thoughts among the "eligibles." Yet the "subliminal" of one or both of them was evidently thinking of this man, from the first. And, also evidently, this was one of the subliminal's little jokes; for, in addition to the trifling obstacle just mentioned (of a wife already existent) there also appears to be, between my young friend and the gentleman in question, a cordial dislike which—says the former—would prevent the planchette-prophecy from "coming true," even if he were the proverbial last man in the world.

Moral: do not ask planchette to prophesy!

In another curious case, the automatist—a correspondent of mine—produced script purporting to come from seven spirits belonging to the planet Saturn. These announced that they were here in a missionary capacity, and had a great revelation to make. (This is quite the usual thing.) For my own amusement and instruction, I inquired concerning the nature of Saturn's ring, and the number of its moons. The spirits showed a sad lack of knowledge—and imagination—for they seemed quite helpless about the ring, and they gave their planet only four moons, instead of ten or so as our astronomers teach. The Revelation was the thing; they were not interested in merely astronomical affairs. In order to introduce this Revelation to the benighted inhabitants of Earth, the medium and myself had been chosen, and were apparently expected to consider ourselves greatly honoured. I was first asked, and then commanded, to arrange a sitting with the medium at the S.P.R. rooms in London. It was casually mentioned that I was to bear all expenses. I suggested that they should give me some ground to go upon, by producing something evidential, in support of their claims. This they disdained to attempt. Instead, they renewed their peremptory commands, breathing out threatenings and slaughter. If I did not obey before a given date, I was to be haled by spiritual messengers before some dread Tribunal. By this time I had got rather bored, the spirits seeming to be a poor lot in the "supernormal" line. Accordingly I intimated, shortly but vigorously, that I had no intention of carrying out their orders. Whereupon they gave me up in disgust.[1]

But let us go a step further. It is proved that planchette (or a pencil in the hand of an automatist who does not need to use the board) will perpetrate mystifications, and that it will sometimes write true matter which is not consciously known to the producers of the script; but, as in Dr. Thornton's case, the facts may be presumed to have been known and forgotten, as they undoubtedly

[1] This automatist told me very frankly, at the beginning, that "they" were often wrong in their statements, and that he had no particular belief as to what they were. He was not a spiritualist.

were in the "Blanche Poynings" case just mentioned. The question naturally arises: Does automatic script ever contain true statements, of specific character, which are inexplicable by chance coincidence or by the normally-acquired knowledge, conscious or subconscious, of the automatist? In other words, is anything evidential ever written which the automatist provably never knew?

It is difficult to prove that any given fact is, and always has been, unknown. I can easily prove that I have some acquaintance with this or that language, but I cannot prove that I am ignorant of others. Negatives are hard to establish. Still, there is good reason to believe that automatic script does sometimes contain evidence of this kind. In such cases it is necessary to resort to the hypothesis of thought-transference. For example, in a case known to me, a man sitting at a distance from two planchette-writers requested the board to write the name of the person of whom he was thinking. The name—an unknown one to the automatists—was written. Evidently, the subconsciousnesses of the planchette-operators had received or obtained the name by thought-reading or telepathy. Such cases are not common, but they are not as rare as might be supposed.

In this case, however, the "sender" of the telepathic message was at least present in the same room. Does it ever happen that the automatists write something which they have provably never known, and which no one present can verify; yet which, on investigation by asking some other person, turns out correct? Yes: even this sometimes happens. The "agent" sometimes seems to be a distant person: and, more curious still, that person is not necessarily trying to "telepath" the facts. It often seems more like mind-reading by the planchettist, than thought-transference from the "agent." For instance, in the following case.

In October 1885, there was a burglary at Netherby Hall, Cumberland, some valuable jewels being stolen. The thieves were caught a few days later, but the jewels were not recovered. Lady Mabel Howard, of Greystoke Castle, Westmorland, who wrote automatically, was asked by friends to try to discover the lost property. She wrote: "In the river, under the bridge at Tebay." It seemed unlikely; but there the jewels were found. If this was not a chance coincidence, we must assume that the mind of one or other of the burglars was somehow tapped.[1] This kind of thing makes it very difficult to exclude a mind-reading hypothesis in cases of alleged spirit messages even of an evidential character.

[1] Full account in *Human Personality*, ii., p. 435, with other cases vouched for by Sir Redvers Buller.

So far, we have been concerned mostly with planchette. But many people can write automatically with a pencil held in the ordinary way, as indeed did Lady Mabel Howard, and as does our medium Watson. No doubt the absoluteness of the automatism varies in different people, and in the same person at different times. There may be complete unconsciousness of what is being written, or there may be a dim awareness, or a consciousness of each word as it comes, with no knowledge of the total sense. It is useless to differentiate at present.

Historically, this phenomenon of automatic writing is no new thing. It is common enough in the annals of religion. Swedenborg practised it, and tells us that his spirits "have sometimes, indeed often, directed my hand when writing, as if it was quite their own"—showing, however, regrettable disregard of truth, "for almost everything they say is made up by them, and they lie." (*Spiritual Diary*. White's *Emanuel Swedenborg: His Life and Writings*, pp. 168, 171.) Further back—taking a case at random—we find another typical instance in Richard Rolle of Hampole, who died in 1349. This mystical worthy was a kind of lay preacher of the Bunyan kind, who wrote prose and verse, in English and Latin. He had studied at Oxford, but gave himself up to the contemplative life

—a dangerous procedure for one of his temperament. "Rolle has ecstasies, he sighs and groans; people come to visit him in his solitude; he is found writing much, 'scribentem multum velociter.' He is requested to stop writing, and speak to his visitors; he talks to them, but continues writing, 'and what he wrote differed entirely from what he said.' This duplication of the personality lasted two hours."[1] Probably the Revelation of St. John the divine was received in somewhat similar way, and many of the instructions to patriarchs, such as Moses (*Exodus* xix., etc.). Certainly automatic productions are allied to the product of genius, psychologically speaking. The more easily and—as it were—unconsciously a work is produced, the better it usually is. It is said that Shakespeare's MS. had no erasures or corrections. Ibsen wrote *Brand* and *Peer Gynt* in an abnormal state; "he would write and write verses day and night—even when half asleep in bed."[2] Goethe said, "Alles ist als wie geschenkt," and many geniuses have had the same feeling, from Caedmon and Langland to Sir Walter Scott, Charlotte Bronte, Dickens, and George Sand.

[1] Jusserand's *Literary History of the English People*, p. 217; *Cambridge History of English Literature*, ii., p. 44.

[2] Haldane Macfall, *Ibsen, the Man, his Art, and his Significance*, p. 108.

But, though the product of this subconscious or unconscious activity may be a work of genius or a revelation (the two are almost the same), it may, on the other hand, be nonsense, or even deceitful, as Swedenborg and others have found. The source, whatever it is, is "part rubbish-heap and part king's treasury." It is therefore necessary to distinguish, and not to accept everything at its face value. This attempt, with regard to automatic writing, particularly on its "supernormal" side, is now being made for the first time with scientific care. The phenomenon is old, but its scientific examination is new. Several people of position, both in the educational and social worlds, have recently developed the power, and are investigating the results in conjunction with the officials of the Society for Psychical Research. Through these automatists, some interesting matter has been obtained; matter which, in my opinion, is not satisfactorily accounted for by any reasonable telepathic hypothesis, and which seems to prove (or as nearly prove as the problem permits) the agency of disembodied intelligence. How such intelligence can act on the material world, on the brain or hand of an automatist, we cannot tell. But, as already remarked, we cannot tell how *our own minds* act on matter. I see my own hand writing, or moving other objects; but

I do not understand how I do it. I make an effort of will, and the thing happens—*voilà tout.* Perhaps Will is the most real thing we can reach.

The next four chapters will give a few examples of the kind of evidence mentioned. Like all other scientific evidence, it is cumulative, and mere selection does not give a good idea of its strength. It is a faggot, not a chain; and of course any separate stick can easily be broken. Accordingly, no single incident can ever be crucial. Even the correct reading of a posthumous letter would not be proof of its writer's continued existence, for if—as it has been claimed—the mottoes inside nuts have been clairvoyantly read, a sealed letter may be similarly deciphered by a medium's supernormal perceptive powers. I say *may be ;* for the motto-reading evidence was not absolutely convincing. I merely wish to point out the impossibility of attaining certainty. An alternative hypothesis is always possible.

I lead up to the famous cross-correspondences by a chapter on the trance-phenomena of Mrs. Thompson, who, however, has now ceased to give sittings. I have purposely avoided quoting from the very latest parts of our *Proceedings*, for these parts, though giving further evidence of the same kind, are perhaps less striking. My aim is not so much to give an up-to-date *résumé* as to select the parts which seem most relevant to the new evidence given in the earlier part of this book, or to the hypotheses which that evidence suggests. I have to thank the Council of the Society for Psychical Research for their kind permission to quote from *Proceedings* and *Journal;* but the accounts should be studied *in extenso* by any one who wishes to form a clear and well-grounded opinion. Miss H. A. Dallas's able little book, *Mors Janua Vitae?* gives a good idea of the evidence which specially suggests the agency of the late F. W. H. Myers, and there are good articles by Mrs. Verrall in the *New Quarterly*, January 1909, and by Mr. G. W. Balfour and Principal Graham in the *Hibbert Journal* of the same date.

CHAPTER XV

THE TRANCE-PHENOMENA OF MRS. THOMPSON

MRS. THOMPSON is a lady who was kind enough to give sittings to a few friends and to others introduced by them, with a view to purely scientific investigation. She was not, and never had been, a professional medium. She showed various forms of "psychic faculty," but the most important form was speaking, and sometimes writing, in a state of trance. Among the investigators who have had sittings with her are Sir William Crookes, Dr. Van Eeden, Dr. Hodgson, Sir Oliver Lodge, Mr. Myers, Professor Sidgwick, and Mrs. Verrall. Dr. Hodgson's half-dozen sittings were almost complete failures; the best sittings recorded are those of Mrs. Verrall, described in *Proceedings S.P.R.*, vol. xvii.

Mrs. Thompson's chief control purported to be her daughter Nelly, who died when a baby. A "Mrs. Cartwright," known to Mrs. Thompson during life, played a secondary part. Sometimes another "spirit" might speak, but, as in the case of Miss McDonald and her control "Sunbeam," it was unusual. As a rule, any messages which the sitter might receive from *soi-disant* relatives of his own, were given by "Nelly," who usually claimed to have received them from the spirits of the relatives in question. The following quotation from Mrs. Verrall's account of her sittings,[1] will give an idea of the kind of evidence produced.

"In what was practically my first sitting with Mrs. Thompson—for I had only been present once before with several other people while she was entranced—Nelly gave me a series of descriptive touches of a dead lady with whom I was intimately acquainted, all of which were true, characteristic, and familiar; but they were not the leading traits in this lady's personality, the points on which I should have seized had I wished to recall her to a third person. Nor was my attention fixed on this particular friend at the beginning, for I had given the sensitive a hair cross and was expecting information about its owner. But the statements of Nelly were definite and accurate, referring to small details of dress—among other things saying that my friend wore a black silk apron trimmed with lace, fastened by an elastic and button round the waist, that this apron had belonged to some one else before her (the lady had often told me that it was her mother's), and that she folded it in a particular way; Nelly also described correctly the lady's objections to the low-necked frocks which my child wore as a baby, and imitated a habit she had of pulling up the child's under-vest to cover her bare neck; she further successfully reproduced a facial trait of this lady, a characteristic movement of the lips, and finally described her as puzzled at the situation, doubtful as to the truth of Nelly's statements that I was really present—all this very characteristic—but engaged in obtaining explanations of the circumstances from Dr. Arthur Myers. There was no sort of reason why Mrs. Thompson should associate the lady in question, had she known

[1] *Proceedings S.P.R.*, vol. xvii., p. 174.

her name, with Dr. Myers; as a fact they had not met more than three or four times, but on those occasions my friend had been in the habit of discussing the problems investigated by the S.P.R. with Dr. Myers, because, as she used to say, his explanations made the things easier for her to understand."

It is possible, of course, that all this was due to "telepathy." That blessed word is very useful, very hard-worked, and very non-explanatory. Let us pass, however, to another case.

The sitters in this instance[1] were Mr. and Mrs. A., Mrs. Verrall acting as note-taker. "Nelly" made a rapid and confused statement, which seemed almost unintelligible. Afterwards, when alone, Mrs. Thompson had a vision of "Mrs. Cartwright," who said that Nelly had made a great confusion between Mr. A.'s relatives, and that she (Mrs. Cartwright) would have to set matters straight. At a later sitting, Mrs. A. present, Mrs. Cartwright replaced Nelly, and the notes of the former sitting were corrected by her. Out of apparently hopeless tangle, order arose; and a series of definite statements was obtained, some of them known by Mrs. A. to be true, others entirely unknown to her. These latter were six in number: one seems incorrect; the other five were as follows:—

(1) It was stated that Mr. A. had a relative, alive, a "rare old lady for knitting"; that she

[1] *Proceedings*, vol. xvii., p. 179.

used to carry about with her a round knitting-basket which contained her "top-knot"—"a cap you might call it, but it was a top-knot."

[Mrs. A. knew an old relative of Mr. A.'s who was a great knitter, but knew nothing of a round knitting-basket or any cap-basket, or any "top-knot." Mr. A. could throw no light on the matter. But his sisters, on being informed of the statement, said that the relative in question, before adopting the old lady's cap, had worn a little knot of black lace which her young relatives called her top-knot, and which she used to take about with her in a round knitting-basket.]

(2) It was stated that Mr. A.'s mother, now dead, "was familiar with the wife of a retired naval officer; you could get information about this." [It was known to Mrs. A. as well as to Mr. A. that his mother had few intimate friends, and of these there was only one whose husband's occupation was unknown to Mrs. A., the lady being a widow when Mrs. A. first heard of her. Mr. A. supplied the information that the husband was "Captain C.," but thought he had been in the army. Mr. A.'s sisters, however, said that he had been in the navy. This Mrs. C. was the only person outside their family group who had visited their mother in her last illness.]

(3) It was stated that Mr. A.'s mother used to wear a white Shetland shawl which was

still in existence in her husband's house; "not in your house (to Mrs. A.), in the other house." [Neither Mr. nor Mrs. A. had any recollection of this, but, once more, the daughters confirmed the statement.]

(4) It was stated that the old lady fastened the shawl with a brooch, which was described in detail. [Mr. and Mrs. A. remembered no such brooch. The daughters, on being questioned, said there was such a brooch, but that the description was wrong in one detail. On finding up the brooch, it turned out that it was the daughters' recollection that was at fault; the communicator's description was correct.]

(5) It was stated that Mr. A.'s mother had possessed a manuscript "receipt" book, still in existence in her husband's house, and that in this book were receipts other than cookery receipts, and in particular a receipt for pomade, or, as the lady herself used to call it, "pomatum." [Mrs. A. knew of the book, but knew nothing of its contents. Mr. A. did not know of its existence. The daughters knew of the book, and said that "pomatum" was the word used by their mother, but they knew nothing of any such receipt. On examining the book, however, a recent entry was found—not indexed, the lady having died soon after making the entry—which gave a receipt for making Dr. Somebody's pomade.]

These five statements are significant because of the following features :—

In all the five cases, the information (*a*) was unknown to one sitter, Mrs. A.; (*b*) was not consciously possessed by the other sitter, Mr. A., though, as to one or two of the details, he may be assumed to have had subliminal knowledge, having known and forgotten, *e. g.* about the Shetland shawl. And, finally (*c*) all the information given was known to the deceased lady from whom the statements purported to come. As to the possibility or likelihood of telepathy from the daughters' minds, it is important to note that these ladies were unknown to Mrs. Thompson, and that they were unaware that references had been made to their family or friends; consequently their thoughts were not directed to reminiscences of deceased relatives. Further, the whole of the facts were not known even to these living though absent persons. The only person who knew *all* was the dead lady herself. "If such experiences as these were numerous, it would be difficult to avoid inferring that the source of information is to be found rather in the one consciousness that knew all the events than in the scattered consciousnesses which can, after all, not supply the whole." [1]

[1] *Proceedings*, vol. xvii., p. 183. The account here given is taken almost *verbatim* from Mrs. Verrall's admirable Report, which may be recommended to the reader's careful study.

Unfortunately, such experiences are *not* numerous, while other experiences are common, which warn us against a too great readiness to accept spiritistic interpretations. It is fairly common, in sittings of this kind, for true information to be given regarding a living person, information which must have been supernormally acquired, but which there is no reason to suppose is in the possession of any deceased person (*e. g.*, the incident relating to Mrs. H. K.'s eyes, already described, p. 56). Such cases, therefore, point to mind-reading or clairvoyance; and it may be that occasionally facts thus acquired are presented in such a way as to suggest a spiritistic explanation which may, nevertheless, be the wrong one.

We now pass to the new kind of evidence to which the name of "cross-correspondences" has been given.

Before his death, Mr. Myers had given some thought to the idea of trying to get a spirit to send the same message through two different mediums. This, it seemed to him, would be an improvement on the kind of evidence previously obtained. Consequently, it was natural to expect, after the death of Dr. Sidgwick and Mr. Myers, that some development of this kind might occur, if these investigators found themselves able to communicate. Dr.

Sidgwick died on August 30, 1900; Mr. Myers on January 17, 1901.

During December 1900, Mr. Piddington (Hon. Sec. S.P.R.) had several sittings with Mrs. Thompson, but there was no mention of Professor Sidgwick, even when his sister (Mrs. Benson) was introduced, with a view to attracting communications. On January 11, 1901, however, the first reference to him was made, quite unexpectedly. "Nelly" said something about "Henry Sidgwick," and, shortly afterwards, a Sidgwick control made its appearance. Not much was said, but the voice and manner, says Mr. Piddington, were extraordinarily lifelike. Another control then appeared, and, speaking on behalf of the *soi-disant* Sidgwick, said:—[1]

> "Eleanor's writing his Life. He doesn't want her to make him 'a glorious personage.' You're to give her that message. He said: 'Eleanor has gone abroad to prepare my Life.'"

We turn now to the trance speech of Miss Rawson (pseudonym), a non-professional sensitive who was, at the time, in the South of France.

In this lady's trance, there appeared for the first time a Sidgwick control, on January 11, 1901—*i. e.*, on the same day as the first Sidgwick control through Mrs. Thompson in

[1] *Proceedings*, vol. xviii., p. 295.

London. The message through Miss Rawson was this :—[1]

"Tell my friend Myers to tell my wife not to put in the whole of the last chapters of the book she is finishing. She will know the passages she feels doubtful about. Tell him it is really I who am here."

The communications, though not identical, are similar, and correct facts are stated or indicated; though these do not count for much, as Mrs. Thompson may easily have known or surmised that Mrs. Sidgwick was writing a Life of her husband. More significant than the *matter*, is the appearance synchronously of a Sidgwick control for the first time through these two sensitives at a great distance from each other.

Further : on January 21, the same control, speaking through Mrs. Thompson with characteristic manner as before, said, "He's (*i. e.*, F. W. H. Myers) not with me. He's not within range at all."

During this sitting, Mrs. Thompson's hand wrote :—

"I don't think Myers is here, or we should see him before the 8th, as E. G. told me [Mr. D., another control] was waiting for him."

On January 23, a Sidgwick control, speaking through Miss Rawson, said :—

"I have not seen my dear friend Myers yet, but I am more thankful than I can say that he has come here. The circle above has been waiting for him, and will with great joy welcome him."

---

[1] *Proceedings*, vol. xviii., p. 295.

Again there is similarity between the messages. Mr. Myers had in life been accustomed to calling the personalities of whom "Mr. D." was one, the "governing group," and this is perhaps what is meant by "the circle above." If so, the messages agree in saying that Mr. D. or his group had been waiting for Myers.

Further confirmatory details might be added, but space does not permit full quotation. It is important to note, however, that the script of Mrs. Thompson, purporting to come from Professor Sidgwick, is a remarkably close imitation of his handwriting, and is quite different from Mrs. Thompson's normal hand. Mr. Piddington showed the script to several people, asking them whose handwriting it recalled to them, but giving no hint. In each case it was unhesitatingly ascribed to Professor Sidgwick.

Mrs. Thompson says that she had never seen any of Professor Sidgwick's handwriting; but this is of course impossible to prove. None of the investigators have any doubt as to Mrs. Thompson's integrity, but it is just possible that she may have seen some of the writing in question, and may have forgotten it. The likeness of the trance-script to the original may thus be due to subliminal knowledge. But this does not explain the cross-correspondences.

CHAPTER XVI

CROSS-CORRESPONDENCES BETWEEN MRS. FORBES, MRS. PIPER, MRS. THOMPSON, AND MRS. VERRALL

AFTER the death of Mr. Myers in January 1901, Mrs. Verrall developed the faculty of automatic writing. Her previous efforts had been failures; but she now made more persistent attempts, which resulted in success. At first the script—mostly in Latin and Greek—was incoherent and non-evidential, but there followed a gradual improvement and clearing in the matter written, along with more tendency to the use of English. Some of the writings were signed, purporting to come from deceased persons; but the majority were unsigned.

On May 8, 1901, between 10 and 10.30 p.m., Mrs. Verrall's pencil wrote a rather unintelligible message in Latin, concluding in English with the words: "*Falsehood is never far away. . . . No power—doing something else to-night.* Note hour."[1] This purported to come from Mr. Myers. On May 11, 1901, was written: "*Before the* 17*th wait.*

[1] *Proceedings S.P.R.*, vol. xx., p. 207.

Rosa Thompson will speak—Lodge will tell you. Wait. Do not hurry date this." From these messages it appeared (1) that a *soi-disant* Myers, writing through Mrs. Verrall's hand about 10.25 p.m. on May 8, claimed to be doing something else, presumably communicating elsewhere, at or about the same time; and, (2) that Sir Oliver Lodge would inform Mrs. Verrall of something that would be said by Mrs. Thompson before the 17th.

The facts turned out to be as follows. Unknown to Mrs. Verrall, Mrs. Thompson was dining on May 8, 1901, with Sir Oliver and Lady Lodge in Birmingham. About 9 p.m. she went suddenly and unexpectedly into trance, and was controlled not only by the usual Nelly, but also by a *soi-disant* Myers. The latter control said something about "falsehood creeping in," and that some one was "calling him" elsewhere; and at the end of the sitting, which concluded at 10.30 p.m., Nelly remarked that some one was calling Mr. Myers. Sir Oliver Lodge's notes of the sitting were given to Mr. Piddington at the Council meeting on May 17, 1901.

The next striking case was a cross-correspondence in which the other sensitive was Mrs. Piper.[1] On January 28, 1902, Dr.

[1] *Proceedings*, xx., p. 213.

Hodgson asked the trance-personality who was communicating through Mrs. Piper, if he could show himself in a vision to Miss Helen Verrall, holding a spear in his hand. The control agreed to try, but asked "Why a sphere?" The misunderstanding was put right, Dr. Hodgson repeating "spear"; and it was promised that the experiment should be tried for a week. At the next sitting, on Febuary 4, the control claimed to have succeeded in showing himself to Miss Verrall, with a "sphear"—so spelt in the trance-writing. This confusion of "spear" and "sphere" is important, in view of what follows. Remembering that Mrs. and Miss Verrall knew nothing of Dr. Hodgson's experiment, it is interesting to find that on January 31, 1902, Mrs. Verrall's pencil wrote the following:—

> "Panopticon σφαιρᾶς ἀτιτάλλει συνδέγμα μυστικὸν τί οὐκ εδίδως; volatile ferrum—pro telo impinget."

The translation of this mixture is not very clear; "panopticon," though not without meaning, is not an extant word. But the idea seems to be something like this:—"*Universal seeing of a sphere fosters the mystic joint-reception. Why did you not give it? The flying iron will hit.*"

Now the phrase "*volatile ferrum*" is used by Virgil for a *spear*; and, consequently, however much of vagueness there may be about the meaning of the whole, there is at least an allusion to a spear, and a definite use of *σφαιρα* (a sphere). It would therefore seem that the Piper control, whoever or whatever he may be, had failed to make himself visible to Miss Verrall as he was requested to do and as he claimed to have done, but that he had instead succeeded—without knowing of the manner of his success—in transmitting the idea of "spear" and "sphere" through Mrs. Verrall's hand. Her script of this day—January 31, 1902—contained other matter, of non-evidential kind, and was signed with two crosses, one of them the Greek cross which is stated elsewhere in the script to be the sign of "Rector," who is the chief control of Mrs. Piper. In view of the possibility of this incident being due to chance, it is important to note that no allusion to a spear had occurred in Mrs. Verrall's previous writings, and that only once had there been any mention of a sphere, in an early and unintelligible piece of script dated March 14, 1901. No case of juxtaposition of the two ideas in the same script had ever occurred before.

The cross-correspondences, however, were not limited to Mrs. Piper as the second automatist. Several good cases occurred, in which a part was played by the script of

Mrs. Forbes (pseudonym)—a lady living in the North of England.

On August 28, 1901,[1] Mrs. Verrall's script had some Latin of which the following is a translation:—

> "*Sign with the seal. The fir-tree that has already been planted in the garden gives its own portent.*"

This script was signed with a scrawl and three drawings representing a sword, a suspended bugle, and a pair of scissors.

On this same day, Mrs. Forbes's script, purporting to come from her son (who had been killed in the South African War), said that he was looking for a sensitive who wrote automatically, in order that he might obtain corroboration for her own writing. This script was apparently produced earlier in the day than Mrs. Verrall's script just mentioned.

The interest of the incident lies in the fact that a suspended bugle surmounted by a crown was the badge of Talbot Forbes's regiment. Further, Mrs. Forbes has in her garden four or five small fir-trees grown from seed sent her from abroad by her son: these she calls Talbot's trees. These facts were totally unknown to Mrs. Verrall. As bearing on the question of chance-coincidence, it is to be remarked that on no other

[1] *Proceedings*, vol. xx., p. 222.

occasion has a bugle appeared in Mrs. Verrall's script, nor has there been any other allusion to a planted fir-tree.[1]

Lest a wrong impression should be given, however, it is necessary to point out that these are perhaps the best cases, and that in one case there was an absolute failure—though introduced by a success—in an incident which claimed to be evidential.

For some time previous to the publication of Mr. Myers's posthumous work *Human Personality*, Mrs. Verrall's script had apparently been trying to give a prediction[2] to the effect that the book would contain an allusion to Plato's *Symposium*, and to Diotima in particular. Also, in Mrs. Forbes's script there had been attempts at the words *Symposium* and Diotima,[3] with unmistakable Greek letters, and the same prediction about the book. Mrs. Forbes did not know the Greek alphabet, had never consciously written Greek letters, had read no translation of the Platonic dialogues, and did not know the name Diotima.

The prediction turned out correct, and thus encouraged the experimenters in another direction. In 1904, Mrs. Verrall's script persistently indicated that a passage from the *Symposium* was enclosed in a sealed envelope

[1] *Proceedings*, vol. xx., p. 224.
[2] *Op. cit.*, pp. 311, 315–16. [3] *Id.*, pp. 246, 315.

which had been left with Sir Oliver Lodge by Mr. Myers.[1] At last it was considered that statements sufficiently definite had been made—considering the success of the previous effort of the scribe—and it was decided to open the envelope. This was done in December 1904: the contents were found to be quite different from what had been given in the script.

This, then, was a complete failure; and those who are hostile to psychical research have made the most of it. But it hardly needs to be pointed out that this failure does not in the least invalidate the many successes in other directions which are now on record. If communication with discarnate minds is possible at all, it is reasonable enough to suppose that such communication is attended with great difficulty, and that we must expect frequent failures and much confusion. We must not overlook or suppress these failures—they must be taken into account in any summing up of the evidence—but, on the other hand, we must not allow them to blind us to the evidential successes of various kinds, or to prejudice us against the possibility of success in a kind of experiment which happens once to have turned out a failure.

[1] *Proceedings*, p. 299.

CHAPTER XVII

CONCORDANCES IN THE SCRIPTS OF MRS. HOLLAND AND MRS. VERRALL

In 1903 there occurred a further development of cross-correspondences. Mrs. Holland (pseudonym), a lady living in India, had been in the habit of writing automatically since 1893, and had occasionally obtained matter which was suggestive of supernormal agency. But she had not made any regular or systematic attempts, and, the society in which she moved being mostly uninterested in these things, she had no encouragement to cultivate the gift. In June 1903, however, she read Myers's *Human Personality,* which greatly impressed her. Soon afterwards, a Myers control purported to communicate in her script, along with Edmund Gurney and Henry Sidgwick—the two friends to whom *Human Personality* is inscribed. Mrs. Holland communicated with Miss Johnson (at that time Secretary of the S.P.R.), sending her portions of her script, and saying how much she herself was puzzled by it.

One of the first indications of supernormality

was the appearance of a description which applied rather closely to Dr. Verrall, with instructions that the script was to be sent to "Mrs. Verrall, 5, Selwyn Gardens, Cambridge." This address is correct. Mrs. Holland was acquainted with Mrs. Verrall's name, through its appearance in *Human Personality*; but that work does not contain her address, which Mrs. Holland did not consciously know. However, it is possible that she may have seen it somewhere, and it is also possible, though extremely improbable, that she had seen a portrait of Dr. Verrall. Automatisms frequently resurrect forgotten knowledge, and this may be a case in point. Another description—of Mrs. Verrall's dining-room—cannot reasonably be explained in this way, but may perhaps be accounted for by chance-coincidence.

A further step was taken, however, in December 1903, and January 1904, when what seems to have been an attempt at similar matter appears in the scripts of Mrs. Holland and Mrs. Verrall—who, it must be remembered, were not personally acquainted at this time. In Mrs. Verrall's script of January 17, 1904, there was a reference to a *text*, in connection, however, with Dr. Sidgwick. On this same day (January 17, 1904) Mrs. Holland, writing in India, obtained some script with similar allusions, and a reference to "1 Cor. xvi. 13" ("Watch ye, stand fast in the faith, quit you like men, be strong"). The scribe also remarks that he is unable to make the automatist's hand form Greek characters, "and so I cannot give the text as I wish."[1] The text in question is inscribed—with the omission of the last two words—in Greek, over the gateway of Selwyn College, Cambridge, which would be passed in going from Mr. Myers's house to Mrs. Verrall's. The road in which Mrs. Verrall lives is named after this College, and there is a mistake in the inscription (the omission of a mute letter) on which Mr. Myers had more than once remarked to Mrs. Verrall. The text, therefore, was likely to be doubly associated with her in Mr. Myers's mind; and it is noteworthy that it turns up in Mrs. Holland's script about a year later, again in connection with Mrs. Verrall, and before Mrs. Holland learnt that there was any significance in its former appearance. This incident, though not very strongly evidential, does at least suggest the personality of Mr. Myers as the possible source of the communication.

It may reasonably be urged, however, that the automatist had supraliminal or subliminal

[1] *Proceedings*, Part lv., p. 234.

knowledge that the text alluded to was over Selwyn College gateway. It is possible that this may be so, but it seems unlikely. Mrs. Holland had never been in Cambridge, and had few friends or acquaintances connected with it. And, even if she knew of the text, it seems improbable that she could know of the special interest which it possessed for Mr. Myers, and of its special suitability as an indication of his identity to Mrs. Verrall. The cross-correspondence part of the incident is not strongly marked, the allusion in Mrs Verrall's script (to a text) being vague, and doubtfully applicable. But a further development occurred, in this direction.

In Mrs. Verrall's script of February 9, 1906,[1] there was a prediction that she would find "two clues" in the forthcoming Life of Dr. Sidgwick. This book was published in March 1906, and Mrs. Verrall found in it two "clues" which seemed to explain certain hitherto incomprehensible allusions in her earlier script—"Hope's vision," "Wanderer on the Way," etc. One of these clues is a letter (quoted in the *Memoir*) from Dr. Sidgwick to his friend Roden Noel, in which he refers to Browning's *La Saisiaz*, in which he found "a kind of repose." The line of thought—the letter continues—is "that on

[1] *Proceedings*, Part lv., p. 316.

moral grounds *hope* rather [than] certainty is fit for us [regarding immortality] in this earthly existence." Mrs. Verrall now read the poem, which to the best of her belief she had not read before, and found in it certain resemblances to the phrases in her script. It is of course possible that she possessed subliminal knowledge of the poem, but it is significant that her script suggesting it, should purport to come from Dr. Sidgwick, who—as shown in the letter just quoted—was specially interested in *La Saisiaz*, and was in special agreement with its line of thought. The letter was written in 1878, and Mrs. Verrall was not acquainted with Roden Noel. The agency of Dr. Sidgwick as communicator is therefore perhaps suggested.

Next, in Mrs. Verrall's script of March 7, 1906, there occurred the following lines:—

"Tintagel and the sea that moaned in pain
And Arthur's mount uplifted from the plain
And crowding towers of quaint fantastic shape
Ah ! never more to see
The ripples dance
Nor hear again the roar
On smitten shore
Where the huge wave rolls on
Amid the salt and savour of the sea."

A copy of this was sent to Mrs. Holland, but the lines suggested nothing to her. It was only when writing the Report that it occurred to Miss Johnson that the lines were very suggestive of Roden Noel's poem *Tintadgel.* The resemblance will be seen by comparing the script with the following quoted lines:—

> "Tintadgel, from thy precipice of rock
> Thou frownest back the vast Atlantic shock!
> Yet purple twilight in cathedral caves
> Moulded to the similitude of waves
> Tempestuous by awful hands of storm
>
> *   *   *   *   *
>
> And therefore Arthur's ancient ramparts range
> From human fellowship to nature, change
> To semblance of the fretted weathered stone,
> Upreared by mystic elements alone."

Mrs. Verrall does not believe that she had seen or heard of this poem until Miss Johnson drew her attention to it in January 1908.

To turn now to the other automatist.

On March 11, 1906, Mrs. Holland wrote automatically:—[1]

> "This is for A. W. Ask him what the date May 26th 1894 meant to him—to me—and to F. W. H.
>
> I do not think they will find it hard to recall but if so—let them ask Nora."

In sending Miss Johnson this script Mrs. Holland remarked that the scribe was not Mr. Myers or Mr. Gurney, and that she hoped the date would have evidential relation to Dr. Hodgson. This showed that the date had no conscious associations for her. As a matter of fact, it was the date of Roden Noel's death. Mr. Noel was not well known to Dr. Verrall ("A. W.") or to Mr. Myers

[1] *Proceedings*, Part lv., p. 319.

(" F. W. H."), but he was an intimate friend of Dr. Sidgwick's. The instructions to " ask Nora " (Mrs. Sidgwick) are therefore appropriate, if we suppose Mr. Noel or Dr. Sidgwick to be the communicator. Further, in this script of March 11, 1906, there are expressions which recall the " clue " which Mrs. Verrall found in the letter from Dr. Sidgwick to Mr. Noel—viz., allusions to " seeking," the " solution of the Great Problem " (which he is still unable to give) and general indications of the idea that he is still *hopeful* rather than *certain*, " though with a confirmed optimism more perfect and beautiful than any we imagined before."

Mrs. Holland's next script [1] begins as follows:—

" (March 14th, 1906.) Eighteen fifteen four five fourteen—Fourteen fifteen five twelve—Not to be taken as they stand. See Rev. 13–18—but only the central 8 words not the whole passage—It does not do to be clearer under existing circumstances.

H. S. [in monogram] R. N. [in monogram] June 1st 1881 (?) "

Revelation xiii. 18, is as follows: " Here is wisdom. Let him that hath understanding count the number of the beast; for it is the number of a man; and his number is Six hundred three score and ten." The central eight word clause of this text is: " for it is

[1] *Op. cit.*, p. 320.

the number of a man." Acting on the hint given in the script, Miss Johnson substituted for the numbers "eighteen, fifteen," etc., the corresponding letters of the alphabet, and found that they formed the name "Roden Noel." Mrs. Holland had not looked up the text, and had no idea what the numbers meant. This incident is not due to any personal interest, for Mrs. Holland had practically no knowledge of Roden Noel, and had read only a few of his Sonnets in a book of selections.[1]

There are a few other possibly relevant details, such as a description, in Mrs. Verrall's script, which correctly applies to Roden Noel, and in Mrs. Holland's script a poetical reference to "rooks," etc.,[2] which may suggest the Cambridge "Backs" and the undergraduate days of Dr. Sidgwick and Mr. Noel; but the main features are given above. As the reader will perceive, the scripts contain nothing that was provably unknown to the automatists, though there is much suggestion of matter which at least was not *consciously* known to them. But, in any case, the cross-correspondences seem significant, and are suggestive of an intelligence apart from, and working through, the automatists.

Another curious incident, analogous to one

[1] *Proceedings*, Part lv., p. 325. [2] *Id.*, p. 321.

just quoted in connection with Mr. Noel, occurred in Mrs. Holland's script of February 9, 1906. The following is the part in question:—[1]

" . . . S j d i b s e I p e h t p o—only one letter further on—

18	8
9	15
3	4
8	7
1	19
18	15
4	14

They are not haphazard figures read them as letters—"

In spite of the hints, Mrs. Holland did not solve the conundrum. Miss Johnson, however, saw that the letters are formed from the name "Richard Hodgson" by substituting for each letter of the name the letter which follows it in the alphabet; while the *numbers* represent the same name by substituting for each letter the number of its alphabetical place.

Dr. Hodgson died in December 1905. Mrs. Holland was no doubt aware of the prominent part which he took in the work of psychical research, but she had no special knowledge of him, or interest in him. The transposition of letters, and the substitution of figures in the second instance, may have been merely a subliminal trick; but it is noteworthy that

[1] *Op. cit.*, p. 304.

Dr. Hodgson, in life, was fond of puzzles and conundrums of all kinds, and that, consequently, this kind of " message " is extremely appropriate and characteristic. Further, there are a few other details in Mrs. Holland's script, which, though not affording evidence of identity, do to some extent support the idea of communication from a genuine Hodgson. There are, for instance, fairly accurate descriptions of his appearance; apparent references to Professor Hugo Münsterberg (" Hugo —H. M.—Minsterberg "), whose book, *The Eternal Life*, had much incensed Dr. Hodgson, who seems to have intended to write a reply to Professor Münsterberg's attacks on pyschical research; and allusions to " Spring on a Boston hill-side " and the redness of the maples (" One clump of maples stands alone —they are outlined against the sunset and the sunset is no redder than they "[1]). Mrs. Holland believes that she had never seen a portrait of Dr. Hodgson, or heard of him before her reading of *Human Personality*; and that she had never heard of Professor Münsterberg. Also, the association of red tints with spring is unlikely for a European, the fact that one of the American maples bears a bright red flower in spring being probably not very widely known on this side.

[1] *Op. cit.*, p. 306.

CHAPTER XVIII

CONCORDANCES IN THE SCRIPTS OF MRS. HOLLAND, MRS. PIPER, MRS. VERRALL, AND MISS VERRALL

MRS. PIPER came to England at the invitation of the Council of the S.P.R., and gave seventy-four sittings between November 10, 1906, and June 2, 1907. The aim of the investigators was to encourage the development of the *soi-disant* Hodgson, Myers, and Sidgwick controls, which had already appeared in Mrs. Piper's trance; and to make experiments in "cross-correspondence." [1] About 120 attempts of this kind were made, the word or idea being suggested by the investigators in eighteen cases, and in the other cases by the trance-personalities. Out of the eighteen, only one was a certain success; of the 102 it is impossible to speak statistically, as the degree of success shades off so gradually. But, as Mr. Piddington says in his Report, some of the cross-correspondences are so specific that chance coincidence can hardly be held to be a satisfactory explanation by any one who will give careful attention to all the facts.

[1] *Proceedings*, vol. xxii., p. 19.

Details concerning manner of communication are not important for our present purpose, which is the summarizing or quoting of evidence; but it may be remarked that, with one exception, Mrs. Piper's sittings were "writing" sittings—*i. e.*, she became entranced, and her hand wrote the communications. With the other automatists concerned, the writing was not accompanied by trance.

The first cross-correspondence described is not strongly evidential, but, being to some extent typical, and being comparatively simple, it serves to lead up to the more complex cases.

In a sitting with Mrs. Piper on November 16, 1906, Sir Oliver and Lady Lodge present, a Hodgson control appeared, and, in reply to Sir Oliver's remark about cross-correspondences, said that he would give "St. Paul" to Mrs. Holland.[1]

As it turned out, "St. Paul" did not appear in Mrs. Holland's script; but in the script of Miss Verrall there are two passages which are possibly relevant. On January 12, 1907, she wrote :—

"the name is not right robbing Peter to pay—Paul sanctus nomine quod efficit nil continens petatur subveniet. [Holy in name—*i. e.*, saint—what she (or he) is doing is of no use (*i. e.*, by itself). Let the point be looked for; it will help."

---

[1] *Op. cit.*, p. 31.

On February 26, 1907, Miss Verrall wrote as follows :—[1]

> "You have not understood about Paul ask Lodge."

Some Latin followed, about calling in the aid of learned men and referring it "to one standard." The only reference to Sir Oliver Lodge in Miss Verrall's script during the period under review, is the one just quoted. The *primâ facie* explanation would be that the control had failed to get his message through in one quarter, but had succeeded when he tried another automatist in the group. It is, however, noteworthy that though "St. Paul" did not appear in Mrs. Holland's script, there *did* appear (December 31, 1906) a reference to St. Peter,[2] a quotation from St. James, and the words, "This is a faithful saying," which appear at least three times in St. Paul's Epistles. This may have been accidental, but, in view of the scripts of Mrs. Piper and Miss Verrall, it is at least suggestive of a partial success. The next incident to be quoted is much more impressive, and also much more complex.

At his sitting of January 16, 1907, with Mrs. Piper,[3] Mr. Piddington suggested to the Myers control that, when he gave a message through two or more automatists, he should mark the message in each case with a distinctive sign,

[1] *Op. cit.*, p. 32. [2] *Id.*, pp. 33, 34.
[3] *Id.*, p. 36 *et seq.*

in order to indicate that they were connected, and were to be compared. "You might put, say, a triangle within a circle, or some simple sign like that," to show that another message similarly marked must be looked for elsewhere. The trance-personality seemed to understand, and promised to carry out the suggestion.

In Mrs. Verrall's script of January 28, 1907, there appeared a clearly-drawn and nnmistakable triangle within a circle, along with a message embodying a successful cross-correspondence. No such diagram appeared in the scripts of the other automatists concerned, though in Mrs. Holland's script of May 8, 1907,[1] there were geometrical figures—a circle, two or three arcs, and a rough approximation to a triangle. The success, therefore, was between Mrs. Piper and Mrs. Verrall only. Now for the cross-correspondence itself.

In Mr. Piddington's sitting of February 11, with Mrs. Piper, the following occurred:—[2]

(Myers communicating.) Did she [*i. e.*, Mrs. Verrall] receive the word
Evangelical.

J. G. P. "Evangelical?"

Yes.

J. G. P. I don't know, but I will inquire. I referred also to Browning again. [I had chosen on December 18, 1906, some words from Browning's *Flight of the Duchess*

---

[1] *Op. cit.*, p. 37.

[2] *Id.*, p. 59. At a later sitting, "Evangelical" was altered to "Evelyn Hope"—the title of a poem by Browning.

for transmission to Mrs. Verrall by Myers,[1] and he had claimed, though wrongly, to have succeeded in getting them written. It is to this that I think "again" refers. J. G. P.]

J. G. P. Do you remember what your exact reference to Browning was?

I referred to Hope and Browning.
Yes (assent to reading as above.)
I also said Star.

Later, Myers$_P$ repeated, "Look out for Hope, Star and Browning."

We turn now to Mrs. Verrall's script.[2]

Jan. 23, 1907.

"Justice holds the scales [underlined]
That gives the words but an anagram would be better
Tell him that—rats star tars and so on. Try this
It has been tried before RTATS rearrange these five letters or again tears
stare
seam
same
and so on
Skeat takes Kate's Keats stake steak.
But the letters you should give to-night are not so many—only three
a s t."

Mrs. Verrall's next script, as below, was done on January 28, 1907.

"Aster [star]
τέρας [wonder or sign]
The world's wonder
And all a wonder and a wild desire—
The very wings of her

---

[1] Myers$_P$ is the *soi-disant* Myers in Mrs. Piper's trance.
Myers$_V$ " " " Mrs. Verrall's script.
Myers$_H$ " " " Mrs. Holland's "
Similarly with the Sidgwick and Hodgson communicators.

[2] *Proceedings*, xxii., p. 61.

A WINGED DESIRE
ὑπόπτερος ἔρως [winged love]
Then there is Blake
and mocked my loss of liberty.
But it is all the same thing—the winged desire
ἔρως ποθεινός [passion] the hope that leaves the earth for the sky—Abt Vogler for earth too hard that found itself or lost itself—in the sky.
That is what I want
On the earth the broken sounds
threads
In the sky the perfect arc
The C major of this life
But your recollection is at fault."

Then followed two drawings—a triangle within a segment of a circle, and a triangle within a circle.

These scripts suggest Browning very strongly, the later one being mostly quotations from *Abt Vogler* and *The Ring and the Book*. *Star* is indicated by "rats star tars" in the first script, and by the "aster" in the second. (Aster="tears, stare" in first script.) *Hope* is suggested by the "hope that leaves the earth for the sky," in which "hope" is misquoted for "passion" (see *Abt Vogler*), as Mrs. Verrall noticed at the time, being familiar enough with the poem. It may be here mentioned that, in Mrs. Verrall's script, an apparently deliberate mis-quotation has occurred more than once, with the aim—so it seems—of emphasizing a special word, as "hope" in the present case.[1]

In connection with the anagram on *star*,

[1] *Op. cit.*, p. 63.

it occurred to Mr. Piddington that he had seen something of the kind when going through Dr. Hodgson's papers in Boston, early in 1906. He therefore asked Dr. Hodgson's executors to search for a piece of paper with "rats arts star" upon it. Such a paper was found; and, in addition to these words, it had upon it—with other odds and ends—the words *stare*, *tears*, and *aster*, which appear in Mrs. Verrall's scripts of January 23 and 28, 1907. This seems to suggest the agency of Dr. Hodgson in regard to these scripts. It was at least clear that he had occupied himself with anagrams on "star" and "tears."

But there was further confirmation as to the intended cross-correspondence, from another quarter. On February 3, Miss Verrall (who had been told nothing of the incidents just described) produced a piece of script containing the word *star*, also a drawing of a star, and the words "therapeutikos ex exoticon" [a healer from aliens]. On February 15, Mrs. Verrall told her daughter, by way of encouragement, of the cross-correspondence between her own script and Mrs. Piper's, substituting, however, other words for the actual ones—"Planet Mars" for *Star*, "Virtue" for *Hope*, and "Keats" for *Browning*. On February 17 Miss Verrall produced script containing a drawing of a five-pointed star, and the following words :—

"that was the sign she will understand
when she sees it
diapason δια πασων ρυθμος [rhythm through all]
no arts avail
the heavenly harmony ως εφη οπλατων [as Plato says]
the mystic three (?)
and a star above it all
rats everywhere in Hamelin town
now do you understand Henry (?)"

Each of these two scripts contains a drawing of a star, and the word "star"; a combination not occurring in Miss Verrall's other scripts of this period. The second script has "arts" and "rats," as well as "star," thus recalling Mrs. Verrall's anagram-script of January 23, and the anagrams on Dr. Hodgson's slip of paper; and the "rats everywhere in Hamelin town" evidently refers to Browning's *Pied Piper of Hamelin.* "Therapeutikos ex exoticon" also perhaps suggests the Piper, who cured Hamelin of its plague of rats, and "there was no guessing his kith and kin."

A noticeable feature of the incident is that Dr. Hodgson had apparently failed to hit on one obvious rearrangement of the letters in *Star*—viz., *Tsar*—and that this form of the anagram is similarly missing in the scripts. Further, the feminine plural πασων (in Miss Verrall's script of February 17) is very appropriate if the "rhythm through all" is an allusion to the concordances obtained through Mrs. Piper, Mrs. Verrall, and Miss Verrall. There are a few other possibly confirming details, but the summary already given will indicate that some explanation beyond chance—and possibly beyond telepathy from the living—is required.

One more case may be quoted, but in briefly summarized form.

At his Piper sitting of February 12, 1907, Mr. Piddington was informed by Hodgson$_P$ that he (Hodgson$_P$) had given "Arrow" to Mrs. Verrall.[1] At a later sitting on February 19, Hodgson$_P$ repeated that he had been trying this, and said "She did get a r I think and stopped there."

In Mrs. Verrall's script of February 11, 1907, there was a drawing of *three arrows*, with the words *tria convergentia in unum* [three things converging to one (point)]. The arrows were drawn as if thus converging. The *word* "arrow" does not appear. But in Mrs. Verrall's script of February 18 there was a drawing of two bows, a drawing of an arch, and the following words:—

> "Blanche de Lys or some such name—but it is all only symlobic [sic]
> It seems to be carvings in stone
> Church architecture or some such thing
> Who wants those drawings? this is quite fresh. I keep trying to say a long word.
> ARCHITECTONIC ARCHITRAVE
> a pointed arch
> I can't get rid of the idea ARCH it obsesses me

---

[1] *Op. cit.*, p. 77.

There has been great confusion here and I do not think anything has been accurately said

Accurate dicta adcuranda sunt [things said accurately are to be attended to.]

But the white arch should give a clue."

In this script, some word beginning with AR is obviously aimed at. Hodgson$_P$ was right when he said (referring to Mrs. Verrall) "she did get a r I think and stopped there."

On March 18, 1907, Mrs. Verrall's script, though still failing to produce the word "arrow," had nevertheless an approximation to the idea, in a drawing of arrows, bows, and a target. Further, in Miss Verrall's script of February 17, there is a drawing of an arrow, with the words "many together," which suggest the three converging arrows in Mrs. Verrall's script of February 11.

With regard to the possibility of telepathy, it is noteworthy that Mr. Piddington did not receive this last-mentioned script (Mrs. Verrall's of February 11) until after his Piper sitting of February 12. Therefore, telepathy from *his* mind cannot be suggested as an explanation of the "arrow" which Hodgson$_P$ said he had given to Mrs. Verrall.

There are two points concerning this script of February 11, which seem worth mentioning, though Mr. Piddington does not draw attention to them, probably fearing over-complexity. They relate to the words "Blanche de Lys." The script, it must be remembered, is trying to give a word beginning with AR, and the scribe purports to be an intermediary of Mr. Myers or his group. Now it happens that "de Lys" was the name under which the family of Jeanne d'Arc was ennobled; and we know that Mr. Myers was greatly interested in the story of the Maid. If his surviving mind were occupied with the letters AR, the thought of Jeanne d'Arc would be likely to arise; and this in its turn would naturally lead to "de Lys." The second point is that "Blanche de Lys" recalls a poem of François Villon's, in which Jeanne is referred to, and which is quoted by Mr. Myers in *Human Personality*, vol. ii., p. 100.

To put the whole thing in a sentence, it seems probable that the letters AR, if given to the living Myers in an association-experiment, would have been likely to suggest the name of Jeanne d'Arc; which, again, would call up "de Lys" and Villon's poem. The script, therefore, is rather characteristic, so far as these points go, of the mind which claims to be communicating. On the other hand, it must be remembered that Mrs. Verrall knew well enough what associations the letters AR would have for Mr. Myers, and that consequently a "subliminal" explanation may suffice. It would have been more satisfactory if the "Blanche de Lys" had appeared in the script of Mrs. Piper.

CHAPTER XIX

THEORY

As already remarked, much theorizing is to be deprecated, the data being insufficient to supply a firm enough foundation. Nevertheless, some idea must be given, however inadequate, of my own personal explanational attitude, so to speak, towards the phenomena which have been described. Otherwise they may remain as an undigested mass in the reader's mental epigastrium, unassimilable, causing discomfort. I will take the facts in order of difficulty, the easiest first.

The phenomenon most easily acceptable, is the one in which Mrs. Napier was given instructions about the papers forgotten by the week-end visitor. This is a simple case of telepathy. I do not say that telepathy is in the least degree understood, nor even that it is the best-established among supernormal facts. For me, it is not. As already stated, I am much more certain of supernormal diagnoses with help of a *rapport*-object, than I am of any other form of supernormality; and I have strong ground for believing that the process is not one of telepathy—certainly not always a reading of the *sitter's* mind. But I recognize that this clairvoyance by *rapport*-object is so *bizarre*, so utterly incomprehensible, that it is not a desirable jumping-off place. Telepathy is nearer to orthodox science. We can fit it in to our mental fabric more easily. The phenomenon of wireless telegraphy (though the analogy must not be pressed, for the mechanism of telepathy may turn out to be entirely different) at least enables us to *believe* that transmission of thought without use of ordinary sensory channels may be possible. Therefore we begin with telepathy, and I say that the incident of the forgotten documents is a simple case of telepathy.

In this case, however, the "agent" was thinking about the documents—thinking hard and anxiously, and connecting them in his mind with Mrs. Napier. It is therefore fairly easy to conceive that this mental activity somehow started a disturbance in the etheric or "metetheric" environment, a disturbance which translated itself into conscious thought in Mrs. Napier's mind, as electrical pulses translate themselves back again into sound, in an ordinary telephone. When we pass to the cases in which Mrs. Napier feels the imminence of visitors before they arrive, the matter becomes a little different. The people are not consciously and anxiously wishing to communicate important information. True, they are no doubt to some extent thinking of the friends they are going to see, and this may start the supposititious "waves"; but there is at least a suggestion that in these cases the percipient's mind is the active one—that it becomes aware, by its own extended range of perceptive power, of the coming events. This is supported by the many cases of precognition in Mrs. Napier's experience, of which I have quoted only one, the others being mostly of a private and family character. These experiences, at least, cannot be explained by telepathy. In so far as they are beyond explanation by inference or by chance, they indicate a wider range of perception, with regard to time. As to the premonition of imminent visitors, it is perhaps preferable to suppose extension of perceptive power with regard to space; for clairvoyance is better established than precognition.

Going a step farther, we seem driven to the conclusion that either this extension reaches to a considerable distance, or that there is an actual spatial change in the location of the perceptive centre, as when Mrs. Napier becomes aware of the condition or the doings of friends at great distances.

An actual change—a real "travelling" of the aware-spot of the *ego*—is suggested by the incident in which an apparition of Mrs. Napier was seen by her father, and by her absolute unconsciousness during the trance. (I mean the unconsciousness of her body; her sister, on one occasion, finding her unconscious, and being unable to rouse her, thought her dead, and was greatly alarmed.) Further, if we are to accept the photograph-case in Chapter I., this would support the same idea of some travelling of the spirit, clothed perhaps in a quasi-material body, invisible to normal eyes, but capable of being photographed, or of being seen by an invalid whose body is wearing thin and allowing the indwelling spirit to see more clearly.

But what of the Anthony Grace and Tom Wyndham incidents? The latter may perhaps have been due to a resurgence of forgotten knowledge, but the former is not thus explicable. Some supernormal agency seems almost established. And I confess that I am unable to explain it satisfactorily by any reasonable supposition of activity on the percipient's part only. Another mind is indicated. And, if one could get over the materialistic prejudices of one's early scientific training, that other mind might seem more likely to be that of the dead Anthony Grace than that of anybody else. We have no reason to suppose that any living person was thinking of the dead man with a view to causing telepathic hallucinations representing him. The *primâ facie* explanation, therefore, seems feasible.

Coming now to the sittings of Mr. Knight with Miss McDonald, we are faced with the same difficulties. Given such supernormal range of perceptive power and of openness to supposed "telepathic impacts," may not all the facts have been conveyed in some supernormal way from Mr. Knight's mind to that of the medium? Undoubtedly he was thinking more or less about his mother, though expecting no evidence; and perhaps the facts given were reverberations of his own thought, dramatized by the medium's subliminal consciousness, which quite possibly believes itself to be the person it is simulating, as when a dreamer believes himself to be somebody else. It may be so. We will return to the point later on.

The next phenomena to be considered are those of the medium Watson. These have already been discussed, and a short survey is all that is required here.

Eliminating fraud, as all the sitters now do, we apply our usual reagents, beginning with our old friend telepathy, or mind-reading as it must in this case be called, for the sitters were usually not thinking the things that were given, and telepathy from subliminal levels is too remote from scientific demonstration to be very seriously considered. How far, then, does a mind-reading hypothesis explain the phenomena?

For many of them it is no doubt adequate, and probably true, or as true as we may expect to get at present. It suffices as an explanation (if we like to call something an "explanation" which is itself so much in need of being explained) of incidents like that of Mrs. Herbert Knight's eyes (p. 56), the disturbed state of the "atmosphere" (p. 132), the correct details about Mr. Frank Knight's business and domestic affairs (pp. 48, 57), and of most of the "sensing" incidents in which the medium gave correct matter regarding a sitter's health, occupation, or interests.

But it begins to be doubtfully applicable when we reach the George Stonor kind of incident, of which Mr. Knight had not thought for a long time; though we certainly have to bear in mind that even forgotten knowledge may be resurrected by planchette-writing and crystal vision. Still, there is a difference between an incident like the Blanche Poynings affair (and presumably the Sir Edward Stanley affair of Dr. Thornton's), there is a difference between these and the George Stonor episode. In the former, there is no necessity to suppose anything supernormal; there is nothing at all puzzling to orthodox psychology. In the latter, there *is*. And, even admitting the possible selective rummaging among forgotten knowledges—a wild assumption, truly, and one which no sane man would accept save as a *pis aller*—even so, it seems difficult to account for such incidents as that of the brown silk dress and the Mrs. Norton and Mary Tranter affairs, there being no evidence that the knowledge in question had ever been possessed by the sitter. And it must be remembered that there is, throughout, the unmistakable and undeniable presence of an intelligence which, whatever it is, is certainly marshalling facts with the definite aim of proving the identity of Mrs. Knight. If that intelligence is Mrs. Knight's, as it steadfastly states itself to be, the whole thing falls into shape; if it is not—if it is the medium's "subliminal"—we are face to face with a problem as difficult as the spirit hypothesis itself—or more so. But there is no scientific ground for believing that the intelligence *is* the medium's "subliminal"; such a guess, it must be admitted, is no more than a rather desperate "bluff," an avoidance of "spirits" by hiding behind a long word which sounds more respectable.

Finally, we come to the automatists of the S.P.R. group. In these phenomena, fraud is excluded on several grounds, and some form of supernormal agency must be admitted, I think, by all unprejudiced students of the full records. Moreover, thought-transference from the sitter or sitters is ruled out. If telepathy from the living is to explain all, we shall have to believe that it can occur *in a very definite and continuous way between people who do not know each other*, as in the earlier script of Mrs. Holland and in some of the trance-speech of Mrs. Thompson. We shall also have to assume a very complicated system of telepathic cross-firing among the automatists concerned, the cross-firing, moreover, occurring at subliminal depths, leaving the normal personalities quite ignorant of all this remarkable activity. I confess that I am unable to accept this. To quote Mr. Lang once more, " there is a point at which the explanations of common sense arouse scepticism." And I do not think that a telepathic theory of this extended kind *can* be called an explanation of common sense. If it were presented on its own merits, and not as a refuge from "spirits," it would be described, by common-sense people, as a piece of uncommon nonsense. And indeed there is little or no evidence in its support, outside of the phenomena which it is invoked to "explain."

Arrived at this point, then, we seem compelled to accept, at least provisionally, the agency of a disembodied mind. For, as in the Watson sittings, there is undeniably some intelligence at work, and there is no scientific ground for placing that intelligence within the mind of any living person. Moreover, the intelligence is certainly of a high order, as is shown by the planning of many of these cross-correspondences. "I care not to whom that intelligence be attributed; but that intelligence and acute intelligence lie behind the phenomena I stoutly maintain" (Mr. Piddington, in *Proceedings*, xxii., p. 35). And Sir Oliver Lodge has said, similarly, that "intelligence and scholarship and ingenuity are being very clearly and unmistakably displayed. Of that we have no doubt whatever. The scholarship, moreover, in some cases singularly corresponds with that of F. W. H. Myers when living, and surpasses the unaided information of any of the receivers." Indeed, some of the communications are strikingly appropriate to and characteristic of Mr. Myers, in many subtle ways; and this psychological kind of evidence, made up of many strokes, some bold, some faint, but all tending to bring out the lineaments of this one personality—this psychoıogical evidence, I say, even apart from anything else, is as impressive as isolated correct facts about the communicator's past life, which is the kind of evidence mostly sought for hitherto. And, adding to this evidence the cross-correspondences, which are also in some instances of characteristic kind—*e. g.*, the anagrams characteristic of Dr. Hodgson, and the Dante, Tennyson, and Browning incidents suggestive of Mr. Myers, there results a body of recent evidence stronger perhaps than anything that has previously been published by qualified investigators, in favour of communication from disembodied human beings.

And, if we admit that these recent S.P.R. results are sufficiently evidential to justify a tentative hypothesis of survival and communication, this throws a retrospective influence on the described phenomena of Mrs. Napier, of Miss McDonald, and of Mr. Watson. If communication does take place, it is possible and even likely that some of the phenomena of these sensitives which we have disposed of as due perhaps to telepathy, may, after all, be genuine communications, as they purport to be. We have discussed them with a constant aim to admit as little of the supernormal as possible, in order to be on the safe side: but it is quite likely that we have been over-cautious, and have labelled "possibly telepathic" many messages which have really come from "the other side." It is very difficult—nay, impossible—to know where to draw the line. The phenomena are, no doubt, of different kinds, shading into each other; and classification at present can only be of the most tentative nature.

While, however, affirming that the evidence for survival is strong, we must nevertheless sedulously avoid dogmatism. The subject is so beset with difficulties, we know so little about the latent or hidden powers of our own minds, that it is dangerous to come to definite conclusions. On any theory, the sensitive's mind may be expected to influence messages; and the "Blanche Poynings" episode proves the subliminal's deceptiveness, or its mistakenness as to its own identity. We can place no reliance on unsupported *claims* to spirit-agency. We must be exigent for *evidence.*

And there may be undiscovered sources of error in the conditions attending experimentation; the evidence, being gathered and presented by fallible mortals, may not give us the truth, the whole truth, and nothing but the truth. Consequently, we must not allow ourselves to be so convinced as to think further evidence unnecessary, or as to become liable to accept evidence which is in itself weak. We must keep up the standard. We may incline to the belief that communication from the "dead" sometimes occurs, but we must not forget that many communications which purport to come from such sources—*e. g.*, in ordinary planchette-script and much trance and "inspirational" speaking—are in all probability correctly explained by subliminal activity. One of the tasks of the psychical researcher or psychologist of the future is to find the farther frontier of the subliminal region, in order to be able to prove that a communication does or does not come from "beyond"—from another order of existence. But, even if the task prove too great, as indeed is most likely—for, as Carlyle said, the attempt of the mind to comprehend itself fully is like the attempt of an athlete to fold his own body in his arms, and, by lifting, to lift up himself—even so, there is still evidence enough to justify even a cautious and sceptical mind in believing that this other order of existence is a fact; that human personality survives the wrench of bodily death, the cosmic scheme widening as the spirit grows; that materialism, at least, is a short-sighted philosophy and a putting of the cart before the horse, spirit being the reality and matter the illusion; that the seen things are temporal, and the unseen things the more enduring. Science is extending our purview into another world, and is confirming the tidings of the poet and the seer :—

> " Who knoweth if we quick be verily dead,
> And our death life to them that once have passed it ? "
>
> (EURIPIDES, *Frag.* 638.)

> " Peace, peace ! he is not dead, he doth not sleep !
> He hath awakened from the dream of life.
> 'Tis we who, lost in stormy visions, keep
> With phantoms an unprofitable strife."
>
> (SHELLEY, *Adonais.*)

No, not unprofitable; we are here for education, and the strife is purposed. We need not grudge the throe. We must learn, nor account the pang. Education and evolution—this is, as Emerson says, the only sane solution of the enigma. Evolution on the other side, as well as on this :—

> " No sudden heaven, nor sudden hell, for man,
> But thro' the Will of One who knows and rules—
> And utter knowledge is but utter love—
> Æonian Evolution, swift or slow,
> Thro' all the Spheres—an ever opening height,
> An ever lessening earth."
>
> (TENNYSON, *The Ring.*)

I say there is evidence enough to justify even a cautious mind in believing this. I do not say that there is evidence enough to prove it. " Proof " is a word that is used with much looseness. In a strict sense, there is no such thing as proof, in inductive problems. To demand " mathematical proof " is to show ignorance of the very nature of the inductive sciences. A theory is justified —therefore proved in the only possible sense of the word as applied to an inductive theory —when it colligates all the facts in a more satisfactory way than any other; but it does not necessarily exclude all other hypotheses. The flat-earth crank is still with us, and supports his belief with rather plausible argument. The anti-evolutionist, also, still abounds, and regards himself as no crank. Yet we regard the spheroid shape of the earth, and the doctrine of differentiation of species by descent-with-variation and natural selection (plus other causes) as "proved." It is only in this sense that the survival of man can be said to be "proved." It is a hypothesis which accounts for the facts better, as some of us think, than any other.

And it does not rest entirely, or even perhaps chiefly, on the facts directly suggesting it, such as veridical apparitions or ostensible spirit-communications through this or that medium. It is not this or that veridical message, but the sum total of established phenomena pointing to a conception of human personality which *involves* personal survival. In other words, we do not so much make an induction of survival from the facts directly suggesting it, as a *de*duction from the personality-conception which the whole of our knowledge necessitates. And it is to be noted that, even if a spiritistic explanation (say, of the phenomena described in this book) is rejected, the alternative hypothesis of telepathy or mind-reading or clairvoyance still points to survival, or at least to a transcendental theory of existence which includes survival as a possibility or a probability. For these phenomena, even waiving "spirits," are not explicable on naturalistic lines. The simplest case of thought-transference seems to lift us out of the category of physical things. The transmission does not fit in with known physical laws; does not seem to weaken according to the law of inverse squares, does not take place in all directions like a physical radiation. These faculties of telepathy, clairvoyance, precognition, do not seem to be products of what Myers called terrene evolution. They are gleams of potencies greater than we know. They suggest that incarnate human beings are spirits manifesting under difficulties—cribb'd, cabin'd and confined by the clogging flesh, by this muddy vesture of decay which doth so grossly close us in.

All this follows, at least as a working hypothesis, if once the Rubicon is crossed, and supernormal phenomena admitted. The only consistent thing for the determined materialist to do is to deny that the phenomena happen. This heroic measure works very well—as it did in my own case—until one's experience is enlarged by running up against some of the facts. Then there is a tussle; for prejudices die hard. But if the investigator will persevere, there is only one end to it. I have never yet known, or heard of, any inquirer who has followed up the research with honest care and vigour, without becoming convinced that things do happen which "common sense" cannot explain. What explanation the inquirer then adopts, depends on his idiosyncrasies. If he has a "will to believe" in personality as a lasting thing, he will be likely to follow Mr. Myers. If not, he may adopt a system of pan-psychism and re-absorption of the individual into the *anima mundi* or into God. "The Drop slips back into the shining Sea." Or he may decline to philosophize, remaining, say, at the position occupied by the late Mr. Podmore.

As for me, I do not greatly care *what* he does. Being no propagandist, I make no attempt to convert any one to my own belief. I state the facts, or what I believe to be the facts, as carefully and accurately as I can, with a little explanation as to why I incline to this or that hypothesis. The reader may then draw his own conclusions—if he feels able to draw any at all, for it is generally found that personal experience is required before much change of belief is effected. I shall be content, therefore, if this book merely helps, on the one hand, to weaken the presumption that "such things can't happen," and, on the other hand, to emphasize the necessity of carrying the most stringent scientific method into these new fields, lest we fall into superstition, which is belief insufficiently evidenced. There has been too much "tumbling up and down in their own conceits" among men, and we now see the ineffectiveness of those performances. Careful observation and experiment, scrupulously accurate recording, and cautious inferring— these are what we now want. It is this scientific method that has yielded such great triumphs in the material world since the time of Bacon; it is possible that the same method, applied in hitherto unexplored regions, may yield an equally important harvest, of another kind.

APPENDIX

The following table may assist the reader in following the narrative concerning Mr. Knight's relatives—

Oliver (*b.* 1784, *d.* 1856) and Nora Upton

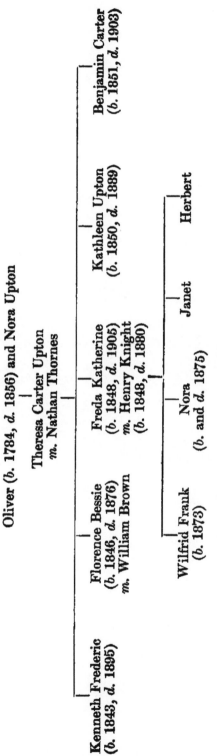

Theresa Carter Upton
m. Nathan Thornes

Kenneth Frederic (*b.* 1843, *d.* 1895)	Florence Bessie (*b.* 1846, *d.* 1876) *m.* William Brown	Freda Katherine (*b.* 1848, *d.* 1905) *m.* Henry Knight (*b.* 1848, *d.* 1880)	Kathleen Upton (*b.* 1850, *d.* 1889)	Benjamin Carter (*b.* 1851, *d.* 1903)

Children of Freda Katherine and Henry Knight:

Wilfrid Frank (*b.* 1873)	Nora (*b.* and *d.* 1875)	Janet	Herbert

It must be remembered that, so far as is ascertainable, no such table as the above is in existence in any place accessible to Mr. Watson.

INDEX

Richard Clay & Sons, Limited, London and Bungay

A LIST OF WORKS

COMPRISING

New Thought
Mysticism
Occultism
Philosophy
Spiritualism
Belles Lettres

Etc.

January, 1911

Including Latest Publications and Announcements.

PUBLISHED BY
WILLIAM RIDER & SON Ltd.
164, ALDERSGATE ST., LONDON E.C.

THE PHILIP WELLBY PUBLICATIONS

The New Thought Library

Crown 8vo. Crimson cloth extra, gilt tops 3s. 6d. net and 4s. 6d. net per volume.

The "New Thought Library" has been designed to include only the best works in this class of literature. No volume will find a place in this series unless it has already an established position in the popular favour. The first nine volumes are now ready.

HAVE YOU A STRONG WILL? How to Develop and Strengthen Will Power, Memory, or any other Faculty, or Attribute of the Mind by the Easy Process of Self-Hypnotism. By CHARLES GODFREY LELAND. Third and enlarged edition, containing the Celebrated Correspondence between Kant and Hufeland, and an additional Chapter on Paracelsus and his Teaching. Price 3s. 6d. net.

CONTENTS —Preface Introduction How to Awaken Attention and Create Interest as preparatory to Developing the Will Faculties and Powers latent in man. Mesmerism, Hypnotism and Self-Hypnotism. Pomponatius, Gassner, and Paracelsus Medical Cures and Benefits which may be realised by Auto-Hypnotism Forethought and its Value Corrupt and Pure Will Instinct and Suggestion The Process of Developing Memory The *Artes Memorandi* of Old Time The Action of Will and Hypnotism on the Constructive Faculties Fascination The Voice Telepathy and the Subliminal Self. The Power of the Mind to Master Disordered Feelings as set forth by Kant Paracelsus, his Teaching with regard to Self-Hypnotism. Last Words

"Why can we not will ourselves to do our very best in all matters controllable by the individual will? Mr Leland answers triumphantly that we can"—*The Literary World*

"An earnestly written work entirely free from charlatanism"—*Birmingham Post*

---

164 Aldersgate Street, London, E.C.

THE GIFT OF THE SPIRIT. A Selection from the Essays of PRENTICE MULFORD. Reprinted from the "White Cross Library." With an Introduction by ARTHUR EDWARD WAITE. Third Edition. Price 3s. 6d. net.

CONTENTS —God in the Trees, or the Infinite Mind in Nature The God in Yourself The Doctor within Mental Medicine. Faith, or, Being Led of the Spirit. The Material Mind *v.* The Spiritual Mind What are Spiritual Gifts? Healthy and Unhealthy Spirit Communion Spells, or, the Law of Change Immortality in the Flesh Regeneration, or, Being Born again The Process of Re-Embodiment Re Embodiment Universal in Nature The Mystery of Sleep Where you Travel when you Sleep Prayer in all ages. The Church of Silent Demand

"The Essays of Prentice Mulford embody a peculiar philosophy, and represent a peculiar phase of insight into the mystery which surrounds man. The essays were the work, as the insight was the gift, of a man who owed nothing to books, perhaps not much to what is ordinarily meant by observation, and everything or nearly everything to reflection nourished by contact with nature "— *A E Waite, in the Introduction*

Under the title "Your Forces and How to Use Them," the Essays of Prentice Mulford have obtained the greatest popularity in America

THE GIFT OF UNDERSTANDING. A Further Selection from the Works of PRENTICE MULFORD. Reprinted from the "White Cross Library." With an Introduction by ARTHUR EDWARD WAITE. Price 3s. 6d. net.

CONTENTS —Introduction. Force, and How to Get it. The source of your Strength. About Economising our Forces The Law of Marriage. Marriage and Resurrection Your Two Memories The Drawing Power of Mind. Consider the Lilies Cultivate Repose. Look Forward. The Necessity of Riches Love Thyself What is Justice? How Thoughts are born Positive and Negative Thought. The Art of Forgetting. The Attraction of Aspiration. God's Commands are Man's Demands

Appendix containing a summary of the Essays of the "White Cross Library" not included in the above volumes

This further selection has been prepared in consequence of the great popularity attained by the first series of Prentice Mulford's Essays, published under the title of "The Gift of the Spirit."

Alter Ego. The Evolution of a Thief, The Honest Man. The Evolution of a Liar, The Truthful Man. The Evolution of a Miser, The Benefactor. The Evolution of an Egotist, The Self-Forgetful Man. The Evolution of a Drunkard, The Self-Possessed Man The Evolution of a Libertine, The Strong Man The Evolution of a Flirt, The Divine Womanly Part III—*Stilling the Tempest* Live in the Eternal, not in Time Affirmation of Being Affirmation for the Morning Affirmation for the Evening Affirmation for Fear of Heredity Affirmation for fear of Death.

EVERY MAN A KING, or Might in Mind Mastery. By ORISON SWETT MARDEN. Price 3s. 6d. net.

"Happily written, with knowledge and insight as well as gaiety and charm."—*Light.*

"Admirable! It is a long time since we have read a book on the fascinating subject of mind's influence over matter, especially in the building of character, with as much pleasure as this has afforded. Characterised throughout by a cheery optimism, the perusal of it is as good as any tonic, and far better than most"—*Pall Mall Gazette*

MENTAL MEDICINE: Some Practical Suggestions from a Spiritual Standpoint By OLIVER HUCKEL, S T D With an Introduction by LEWELLYS F. BARKER, M D Price 3s. 6d. net.

SUMMARY OF CONTENTS—The New Outlook for Health. The Unique Powers of Mind. The Spiritual Mastery of the Body. Faith as a Vital Force. The Healing Value of Prayer Glimpses of the Subconscious Self. The Training of the Hidden Energies The Casting Out of Fear The Cause and Cure of the Worry Habit The Gospel of Relaxation. Work as a Factor in Health Inspiration of the Mental Outlook. Best Books for Further Reading.

"Unusually bright and stimulating discourses"—*The Scotsman*

"A book of common sense and reason, and its logic is unassailable in almost every chapter."—*Pall Mall Gazette*

NEW VOLUME.

SELF-CONTROL, AND HOW TO SECURE IT (L'Education de Soi-même). By Dr. PAUL DUBOIS, Professor of Neuropathology in the University of Berne; Author of "The Psychic Treatment of Nervous Disorders," "The

Influence of the Mind on the Body," etc. Authorized Translation. By HARRY HUTCHESON BOYD. 337 pp., 4s. 6d. net.

"'*Man is the only animal who does not know how to live,' I said one day, after listening to the grievances of my patients*" In these words the learned Genevese doctor introduces a book, the object of which is to correct this defect of the human race Dr Paul Dubois' extensive experience of all sorts and conditions of men, and of their physical, mental and moral ailments, renders him well qualified for the position of confidential adviser to the world in general on so important a subject. The aim of this book, which has already won a well-deserved popularity on the Continent and in America, is to point out the road indicated by a due regard for consideration of physical and moral well-being to those who, without some such aid, are only too liable to take the wrong turning for lack of the necessary guidance and worldly wisdom The book covers such varied subjects as The Conquest of Happiness, Conscience, Education, Egoism and Altruism, Indulgence, Moderation, Courage, Idealism, etc , etc

"Eighteen wise and lively essays on subjects relating to common life, all entirely deserving attention for their bright wisdom, and easy to read because of their simple and happy style"—*Light*

"A thoroughly wholesome and sound book"—*T P S Book Notes*

"This is a manual of self-culture a series of brilliant essays, bold in conception, sympathetic in spirit, and eminently serviceable in substance"—*The Health Record*

THE GIFT OF THE SPIRIT. Pocket Edition (5in × 3in). Leather, gilt, 2s. 6d. net.

Mysticism

ON A GOLD BASIS. A Treatise on Mysticism. By ISABELLE DE STEIGER, Translator of "The Cloud upon the Sanctuary" by ECKARTSHAUSEN. Crown 8vo, cloth, gilt, 3s. 6d. net.

"Unlike other Western writers, Isabelle de Steiger has been at great pains to understand aright what the principles as applied in Eastern philosophy are, and the result is that we have a book which is reliable from every point of view—reliable as regards the information it contains, reliable as regards the deductions made therefrom, and reliable as an authoritative exposition of all that is best and true in the science of mysticism Eastern scholars as well as Western scholars will benefit immensely by a perusal of this excellent book."—*The Indian Review*

"One of the most fruitful and suggestive inquiries into modern problems of thought and life which has been made . As a treatise on mysticism it touches the subject at all points, a new light appearing as each facet is brought into view, a kaleidoscopic enchantment At whatever page you may choose to open up the book, there is something new and suggestive."—"Scrutator" in *The Occult Review*

THE CLOUD UPON THE SANCTUARY. A Text Book of Christian Mysticism. Third Edition. Revised and Enlarged. Crown 8vo, xxxix. + 144 pp., 3s. 6d. net. By COUNCILLOR KARL VON ECKARTSHAUSEN. Translated and Annotated by ISABELLE DE STEIGER, and with an Introduction by ARTHUR EDWARD WAITE.

The fullest and clearest exhibition of the Doctrine of a Secret Holy Assembly within the Christian Church.

"I can very cordially recommend to all who are interested in religious mysticism 'The Cloud upon the Sanctuary.' . . . Not only is Eckartshausen's text of the highest curiosity and interest, but the 'critical apparatus' furnished by the translator, by Mr. Brodie-Innes, and by others, will prove most helpful to the student, and Mr A. E. Waite's 'Introduction,' with its historical study of the author, and its store of recondite learning, adds the finishing touch to this valuable edition of a very valuable and singular work."—*T P's Weekly*

THE HIDDEN WAY ACROSS THE THRESHOLD; or, The Mystery which hath been Hidden for Ages and from Generations. An explanation of the concealed forces in every man to open THE TEMPLE OF THE SOUL, and to learn THE GUIDANCE OF THE UNSEEN HAND. Illustrated and made plain, with as few occult terms as possible, by J. C. STREET. Large 8vo. With Plates, 12s. net.

The writer of this book, it is admitted, has enjoyed access to sources of information not commonly open to mankind in its present state of development.

STEPS TO THE CROWN. BY ARTHUR EDWARD WAITE. Foolscap 8vo, buckram, 2s. 6d. net.

"Mr. Waite has presented his philosophy of life in a series of aphorisms. The author of this volume is well known as one of the best living authorities on the history of mysticism, and the point of view here maintained is that of an initiate. Nature is regarded as an enemy—a sleeping serpent Man's highest destiny lies—as St Augustine taught many centuries ago—in his ultimate union with the Divine Nature. The great renunciation is to surrender that which matters nothing in order that we may possess everything. There are several hundreds of aphorisms in this slender volume, all of them terse and pregnant."—*The Tribune.*

NOTES ON THE MARGINS. Being Suggestions of Thought and Enquiry. Five Essays by CLIFFORD HARRISON. Crown 8vo, 3s. 6d. net.

CONTENTS.—An Enquiry into Mysticism, The Illusion of Realism. The Lines of Coincidence. Arrest or Advance? The Lost Riches of the World.

"Perhaps the best and most readable introduction to the under standing of the true spirit and meaning of Occultism, or as the author prefers to call it, Mysticism, which we could offer to any one desirous of information on the subject"—*Theosophical Review.*

JUST PUBLISHED.

THE WAY OF THE SOUL. By WILLIAM T. HORTON, Author of "The Book of Images." A Legend in Line and Verse, depicting the Soul's Pilgrimage through matter. With Foreword by RALPH SHIRLEY. 48 full-page Symbolical Illustrations. In artistically designed blue cloth binding, black and gold lettering, with symbolical design. Crown 4to, gilt tops, 224 pp, 6s. net.

In a series of fine line drawings and simple descriptive verse Mr. Horton has given a symbolical rendering of the ever-essential, yet ever-changing, problem of the progress of the Soul-form under the rulings of circumstance as it is planned and directed by the Spirit. Not only is the book a mystically conceived poem, but, reading between the lines, one may find a sane and useful guide to living the everyday life.

NOW READY.

ANCIENT MYSTERIES AND MODERN REVELATIONS. By W. J. COLVILLE, Author of "Fate Mastered," "Life and Power from Within," etc., etc. With Portrait of the Author. Crown 8vo, 366 pp., cloth gilt, 3s 6d. net.

Selection of Contents.—Bibles under Modern Search-light—How Ancient is Humanity on this Planet?—Egypt and its Wonders—Apollonius of Tyana—Five Varieties of Yoga—The Message of Buddhism—Ancient Magic and Modern Therapeutics—Andrew Jackson Davis, a Nineteenth Century Seer—The Latest Views on Evolution—Spiritualism and the Deepening of Spiritual Life—The Divine Feminine—Psychopathic Treatment; or, Suggestive Therapy in Practical Application.

AZOTH; OR, THE STAR IN THE EAST (A New Light of Mysticism). Embracing the First Matter of the Magnum Opus, the Evolution of Aphrodite-Urania, the Supernatural Generation of the Son of the Sun, and the Alchemical Transfiguration of Humanity. By Arthur Edward Waite. Cloth gilt, 239 pp., imp. 8vo, 5s. net.

Contents.—Preface—The Gate of the Sanctuary—Introduction—The Outward Man—The Inward Man—Appendices.

This book deals with the life of the mystic in a thorough and illuminating manner. The various phases of mysticism, its philosophy, its method, its discipline and its glory, are treated *seriatim* in a volume which must be regarded as of great value to all students of mysticism.

Psychic Phenomena and Spiritualism.

IN PREPARATION.

THE PSYCHOLOGY OF THE UNKNOWN. (La Psychologie Inconnue). A Contribution to the Experimental Study of the Psychic Sciences. Translated from the French of Emile Boirac, Correspondent of the Institute, Rector of the Academy of Dijon. Demy 8vo., cloth gilt, 6s. net.

READY IN FEBRUARY.

NEW EVIDENCES IN PSYCHICAL RESEARCH. By J. Arthur Hill. With Introductory Note by Sir Oliver Lodge, F.R.S. Crown 8vo, cloth gilt, 224 pp., 3s. 6d. net.

CHRISTIANITY AND SPIRITUALISM (*Christianisme et Spiritualisme.*) By Léon Denis Translated by Helen Draper Speakman. Crown 8vo, 3s. 6d. net.

Contents —The History of the Gospels The Secret Doctrine of Christianity Intercourse with the Dead The New Revelation

The writer contends that Spiritualism offers tangible proofs of immortality, and thus carries us back to the pure Christian doctrines.

"A book possessing deep and obvious interest for many thoughtful minds"—*T P's Weekly*

HERE AND HEREAFTER (*Après la Mort*). Being a Scientific and Rational Solution of the Problems of Life and Death, and of the Nature and Destiny of the Human Ego in its Successive Lives Translated by George G. Fleurot from the French of Leon Denis, author of "Christianity and Spiritualism." Second edition, revised, cloth gilt, crown 8vo, 352 pp., 3s 6d. net.

An able and luminous account of the phenomena and doctrines included under the term "Spiritualism," their relation to modern science and their influence on conduct The present volume is a new and enlarged edition of the original work, the popularity of which, across the Channel, may be gauged by the fact that it has already run into its twenty-second thousand

"A wonderful book, which should appeal to every intelligent and civilized person, of whatever rank or nationality"—*The Lady*

"It deals with profound subjects in a simple way, and while the most experienced will find instruction in it the beginner will find no difficulty in the attempt to master it from the first page to the last."

—*Light.*

EVIDENCE FOR A FUTURE LIFE. A Translation of Gabriel Delanne's Important work "L'Ame est Immortelle." By H A. Dallas, Author of "Gospel Records Interpreted by Human Experience" Demy 8vo, 5s. net.

This work has been accepted by all Spiritualists as an unequalled summary of the most notable phenomena of modern times, chiefly with reference to the "perisprit" or fluidic body, by which man is brought into direct contact with the unseen universe

"He makes out an extremely strong case"—*Light*

"It covers the whole field of spiritualism in a perfectly serious, rational and scientific manner."—*Daily Express.*

MORS JANUA VITAE? A discussion of certain communications purporting to come from FREDERIC W. H. MYERS. By H. A. DALLAS, with Introduction by PROFESSOR W. F. BARRETT, F.R.S Crown 8vo., cloth gilt, 2s. 6d. net.

No discussion within the sphere of Psychical Research during recent years has attracted more public attention than that relating to the alleged communications of the late Frederic W H. Myers—principally by the method described as cross correspondence—with his erstwhile colleagues of the S P.R The object of this book is to put before the reading public who are interested in the latest developments of psychic investigation the main facts of the evidence in this remarkable case

"Has dealt with her material in a lucid and interesting way."
—*The Christian Commonwealth.*

"We can cordially praise Miss Dallas's exposition."—*The Guardian.*

"A timely little book."—*Light.*

HIGHLAND SECOND SIGHT, with prophesies of Coinneach Odhar and the Seer of Petty. Introductory Study by REV. WM. MORRISON, M.A. Edited by NORMAN MACRAE. Crown 8vo, 202 pp., cloth bound, leather back, 3s. 6d. net.

It is hoped that this book will prove as helpful to the serious student as, it is believed, it will be welcome to the general reader, not in the light of the superstitious or the merely curious, but as a subject of particular interest in view of present day research in matters psychological.

COLLOQUIES WITH AN UNSEEN FRIEND Edited by WALBURGA, LADY PAGET. Crown 8vo, White Linen, 3s. 6d. net.

CONTENTS —Reincarnation Atlantis Conditions of Communication with the Invisible Historical Sketches Humanitarianism and the Advance of the world The French Revolution and Secret Societies War and Politics Scraps St Francis

This volume consists of a remarkable series of communications, recorded by a highly developed medium

" Always daring and often original "—*The Planet*

THE PAST REVEALED: A Series of Revelations concerning the Early Scriptures. Recorded by E C. GAFFIELD, Author of "A Series of Meditations," and "A Celestial Message." Crown 8vo, blue cloth, gilt tops, 309 pp., 2s. 6d. net.

" As we read this vivid, profound, and yet simple exposition of human life in long-departed ages, we can indeed feel that a veil has been lifted, and some portion of truly gnostic information has been unfolded to the world "—W J COLVILLE

THE WATSEKA WONDER: A narrative of startling phenomena and an authenticated instance of spirit manifestation, throwing a remarkable light on certain of the phenomena of multiple personality. By E. W STEVENS, M.D , with introduction by J M. PEEBLES, M.D. Paper covers 1s. 6d. net.

READY IN FEBRUARY.

Demy 8vo About 600 pp , 10s 6d net

PSYCHICAL AND SUPERNORMAL PHENOMENA. Being a translation by DUDLEY WRIGHT of "Les Phénomènes Psychiques," the new and very notable work of DR PAUL JOIRE, Professor at the Psycho-Physiological Institute of Paris, President of La Société Universelle d'Études Psychiques.

CONTENTS—Psychical Phenomena generally considered Externalisation of Sensibility Spontaneous Phenomena Multiple Personalities Abnormal Faculties in Hypnotic Subjects Abnormal Dreams Phenomena of Lucidity and Externalisation observed in Fakirs or Oriental Sorcerers Haunted Houses Telepathy

Crystal Gazing Clairaudience Typtology Automatic Writing and Lucidity Thought Photography Movement of Objects without Contact Levitation Eusapia Paladino Materialisations General view of Psychical Phenomena

READY IN FEBRUARY.

DEATH: ITS CAUSES AND PHENOMENA. By HEREWARD CARRINGTON and JOHN R MEADER 8s 6d. net

CONTENTS

REINCARNATION AND CHRISTIANITY. A discussion of the relation of orthodoxy to the reincarnation hypothesis. By a Clergyman of the Church of England. Crown 8vo, stiff boards, 96 pp, 1s. net

The unique characteristic of this book is that it is the first attempt ever made in literary form to justify the theory of Reincarnation from the standpoint of Christianity The writer attempts to prove that even to the stickler for orthodoxy, there is nothing inconsistent, or out of harmony with the teachings of the church, in the avowal of a belief in the evolution of the soul through the tenancy by it of a succession of physical bodies He quotes Jesus Christ Himself as pointedly refraining from disavowing such a belief, and instances the declared adherence to the doctrine of a number of early Christian Fathers He shows that it is a mistake to suppose that Reincarnation was ever condemned at any authoritative Council of the Church, and proceeds to argue that many of the Christian's greatest difficulties are solved by its acceptance

"A brief but thoughtful defence of the doctrine that each soul is reaping the consequences of a past"—*The Times*

"A well-written volume."—*The Scotsman*

"He grapples with the difficulties which an orthodox Christian might raise His very fair and temperate argument"
—*The Quest*

"It will fulfil a most useful function"—*T P S Book Notes*

Philosophy.

JESUS: THE LAST GREAT INITIATE. Translated from "Les Grands Initiés" of Édouard Schure, by F. Rothwell, B.A. Crown 8vo, cloth, 2s net.

"The Light was in the world, and the world was made by it, but the world knew it not"—John i 10

"When a man listens to the Divine Call a new life is created in him, now he no longer feels himself alone, but in communion with God and all truth, ready to proceed eternally from one verity to another In this new life his thought becomes one with the Universal Will"

"Always suggestive and often eloquent"—*The Scotsman*

KRISHNA AND ORPHEUS, the Great Initiates of the East and West. By Édouard Schure. Translated by F. Rothwell, B.A. Crown 8vo, cloth, 2s. net

"The work is learned and interesting"—*The Scotsman.*

"Would get hold of the imagination of the dullest"
—*St James's Gazette*

"An admirable translation"—*Glasgow Herald*

PYTHAGORAS, and His System of Philosophy, (The Delphic Mysteries.) By Edouard Schure. Translated by F. Rothwell, B.A. Crown 8vo, cloth, 2s. net.

"Know thyself, and thou wilt know the Universe and the Gods" — A thoughtful history and exposition of the great teacher" *The Scotsman*

"In this excellent translation the reader is familiarised with the life and philosophy of Pythagoras"—*The Daily Express*

HERMES AND PLATO. The Mysteries of Egypt and the Mysteries of Eleusis, by ÉDOUARD SCHURÉ Translated by F. ROTHWELL, B.A. Crown 8vo., cloth, 1s. 6d net.

"Happy is he who has passed through the Mysteries He knows the source and the end of life"—PINDAR

"M Schure has presented a picture of ancient religious indoctrination that will give an excellent general idea of the scope and significance of the Greek and Egyptian mysteries"—*Light*

"An interesting essay on the occultism of the ancient world" —*The Scotsman*

RAMA AND MOSES. The Aryan Cycle and the Mission of Israel. Translated from "Les Grands Initiés" of ÉDOUARD SCHURÉ. by F. ROTHWELL, B.A. Crown 8vo cloth, 2s. net. N.B.—This volume completes the series.

"M Schure brings to his work a wonderful picture-making faculty"—*T P S Book Notes*

"The work will be of great value to the serious student of the origin of religions"—*Annals of Psychical Science*

WITH THE ADEPTS: An Adventure among the Rosicrucians. By Dr. FRANZ HARTMANN. New and Revised Edition. Crown 8vo, cloth gilt, 180 pp., 2s. 6d. net

"This interesting narrative of a psychic experience" —*The Theosophist*

THE BOOK OF THE SIMPLE WAY. By LAOTZE ("The Old Boy") A New Translation of "The Tao-Teh-King." With Introduction and Commentary by WALTER GORN OLD, M.R.A.S., Crown 8vo, cloth, 2s. net

"Laotze remains a prince among philosophers and is still as good reading as he was some five or six centuries B C"—*The Times*

"An excellent translation of the teachings of this ancient sage As an editor and expositor Mr. Old is both well-informed and sympathetic"—*Glasgow Herald*

OBERMANN. By ÉTIENNE PIVET DE SENANCOUR Translated from the French, with Biographical and Critical Introduction by ARTHUR EDWARD WAITE. Crown 8vo, 423 pp., 6s net, ornamental cloth, gilt tops.

"A Spiritual Autobiography, rich in the invitation to think, alive with the quest of truth, and yet full of speculative unrest The value of this edition is greatly enhanced by the critical appreciation with which Mr Waite has enriched a book that deserves to be much more widely known"—*The Standard*

"An excellent translation."—*The Times*

"Mr Waite must be well known as a learned and enchanting Mystic, even those who are not mystics or even thyrsus-bearers hold him in respect We are therefore not surprised that he treats *Obermann* as 'A great book of the soul,' and De Senancour as a man of vision 'belonging at his best to eternity'"—*The Daily Chronicle.*

THE LIFE OF LOUIS CLAUDE DE SAINT-MARTIN, the Unknown Philosopher, and the Substance of his Transcendental Doctrine. By ARTHUR EDWARD WAITE. Demy 8vo, 464 pp, 6s net.

CONTENTS —Book I Louis Claude de Saint-Martin Book II Sources of Martinistic Doctrine Book III The Nature and State of Man Book IV The Doctrine of the Repairer Book V The Way of Reintegration Book VI Minor Doctrines of Saint-Martin

Appendices —1 Prayers of Saint-Martin 2 Metrical Exercises of Saint-Martin 3 Bibliography of the Writings of Saint-Martin Index

"The feet of Saint-Martin are on earth, but his head is in heaven" —JOUBERT

"A profoundly spiritual view of the world, an interpretation of Christianity which, though free, is also suggestive, and a handling of the moral problems of life which is marked by insight and power"—*Scotsman*

"Men of distinction have spoken of Louis Claude de Saint-Martin with respect and even admiration as a modern mystic who had more to recommend him than obscurity and extravagance"—*The Times*

PSYCHIC PHILOSOPHY, AS THE FOUNDATION OF A RELIGION OF NATURAL CAUSES. By V. C. Desertis. With Introductory Note by PROFESSOR ALFRED RUSSEL WALLACE, O.M., D.C.L., LL.D. F.R.S. New edition, largely re-written, cloth gilt, gilt tops, crown 8vo, 421 pp., 4s. 6d. net.

CONTENTS —Introductory Note and Preface —Part I. The Bases of Experimental Fact Part II. Theory and Inferences Part III Practical Mysticism

"The book is replete with sound, scholarly, cogent and practical reasoning, on the scientific and religious, as well as on the psychic side, and may well be taken as a treasury of arguments proving that the spiritual philosophy is a necessity for the future well-being of the world."—*Light*

"There is much in this volume which we have found both helpful and stimulating, and with which we are in entire agreement."

—*The Academy*

"Temperately and carefully written, and is in every way superior to the average spiritualistic publication "—*T.P.'s Weekly.*

"In every way worthy of study."—*Christian World.*

THE WISDOM OF PLOTINUS. A Metaphysical Study, by C. J. WHITBY, M.D. 120 pp. crown 8vo, cloth gilt, 2s. net.

A Treatise on the metaphysical doctrines of the great Neoplatonic Philosopher.

CONTENTS —Life of Plotinus Ancient and Modern Methods Neo-platonism Matter The Universe Individuality The Problem of Evil Providence and the Individual. Demons and the Demonic Faculty Concerning Love and Emotions Substance or Corporal Essence. Time and Eternity Doctrine of the Soul Individuality. Incarnation or Descension. Intelligence, and the Intelligible World. Primal Categories or Elements of the Notion. Universal Number. Number and Unity. Time and Space in Eternity. Ideal Functions of Time and Space Universal Differentiation Intelligence and the One. The One Potential Import of the Doctrine of Unity

"For the professed student of philosophy, Plotinus still remains the most important of the Neoplatonists, and his theories cannot be neglected. Mr. Whitby has presented them in an admirably concise and lucid form, and for metaphysicians his little volume will be indispensable "—*Globe.*

"A short but useful exposition, carefully analysed, of the life and teaching of the great third century Neoplatonist"—*Times*

"We can confidently recommend Dr Whitby's admirable study to lovers of the greatest intellect of the first Platonic renascence A very good book to serve as an introduction to a first-hand study of the immortal Enneads"—G R S MEAD in the *Theosophical Review.*

RATIONAL MEMORY TRAINING. By B. F. AUSTIN, M.A., B.D, Ex-Principal of Alma Ladies' College, St. Thomas, Ontario. Author of "Woman, Her Character, Culture and Calling," "Glimpses of the Unseen," "Success and How to Attain It," and Editor of "Reason." 147 pp. crown 8vo, 1s. 6d. net, brown paper covers.

A series of articles on Memory, its Practical Value, its Phenomenal Powers, its Physiological Basis, the Laws which govern it, the Methods of Improving it, Attention, Association and Arrangement of Ideas, Causes of Defective Memory, Mnemonics, their Use and Abuse, etc, etc, with Hints and Helps in Memorizing Figures, Lists of Words, Prose and Poetic Literature, New Languages, etc

THE THREE GREAT TIES. The Humanities, the Amenities, the Infinities. By J E. A. BROWN, author of "The First Four Things," &c Royal 18mo Canvas, 1s. 6d. net.

"These essays have charm, insight, and suggestiveness, reminding one of the late Mr Hammerton in his 'Intellectual Life' Grace and Truth are here beautifully blended"—*Western Morning News.*

"Abounds in practical wisdom"—*Glasgow Herald*

THOUGHTS ON ULTIMATE PROBLEMS: A Study of Two Theodicies. By W. F. FRANKLAND. Crown 8vo, paper cover, 1s. net.

"There is packed within this pamphlet of twenty pages sufficient matter to fill almost as many volumes Thinkers all the world over will hail the present work as a logical and stimulating contribution to the literature of idealistic philosophy"—*New Zealand Mail*

THE WORLD WE LIVE IN. By E. A. BRACKETT, with Portrait of the Author. Crown 8vo, $8\frac{1}{4}$in. × $5\frac{3}{4}$in., 121 pp., cloth gilt, gilt tops, 2s. net.

This book gives a singularly clear exposition of the meaning of life as seen through the spectacles of a believer in Spiritualism

"In view of his long study of such questions, his remarks on spiritualism, mesmerism and kindred phenomena are deserving of respect."—*Sunday Times*.

"Thoughtful, picturesque and refreshing"—*The Scotsman*.

YOGA OR TRANSFORMATION. A comparative statement of the various religions and dogmas concerning the Soul and its destiny, and of Akkadian, Hindu, Taoist, Egyptian, Hebrew, Greek, Christian, Mohammedan, Japanese and other Magic. By WILLIAM J. FLAGG. Royal 8vo, 376 pp., cloth gilt, cheaper edition, 6s. net.

OCCULT SCIENCE IN INDIA AND AMONG THE ANCIENTS. With an account of their mystic initiations and the history of Spiritism. By LOUIS JACOLLIOT. Translated from the French by WILLARD L. FELT. Royal 8vo, 276 pp., cloth gilt, gilt tops, cheaper edition, 6s. net.

THE ZODIACUS VITÆ of MARCELLUS PALINGENIUS STELLATUS. An Old School Book. Edited and Abridged by FOSTER WATSON, M.A., Professor of Education in the University College of Wales, Aberystwyth. Crown 8vo. 2s. net.

"The book is entitled 'The Zodiac of Life,' because a life led in accordance with its teachings is as glorious as the sun travelling through the signs of the Zodiac."—THOMAS SCAURINUS (Old writer)

"Palingenius writes as an alchemist and astrologer. . . keenly desirous to give a spiritual application to all physical theories"

—*Times*.

MATTER, SPIRIT AND THE COSMOS Some Suggestions towards a Better Understanding of the Whence and Why of their Existence. By H. STANLEY REDGROVE, B.Sc. (Lond.), F.C.S., Author of "On the Calculation of Thermo-Chemical Constants." Crown 8vo, cloth gilt, 2s. 6d. net.

"Another evidence of the revolt that seems to be gradually rising against the materialism of the late nineteenth century As a student of science, the author may be considered as at least an unprejudiced advocate for the reality of spirit"—*The Scotsman*

"The thoughtful reader who is not satisfied with what materialism has to offer him will find food for reflection in this book the author's conclusions are well stated, and are based upon careful reasoning and accurate interpretation"

—*Chemical News, edited by Sir Wm Crookes*

Higher Life Handbooks.

Crown 8vo. Uniformly bound in handsome dark green cloth. Gilt ornamental design and lettering.

LIFE AND POWER FROM WITHIN. By W. J. COLVILLE, Author of "The Law of Correspondences," "Elementary Text-Book of Mental Therapeutics," etc., etc. 189 pp., 2s. 6d. net.

"Written in the fluent, simple and direct style characteristic of the author"—*T P S Book Notes*

"It can be strongly recommended to all who wish to go beneath the surface of things, and get at the springs of life"—*The Pioneer*

THE LAW OF THE RHYTHMIC BREATH, TEACHING THE GENERATION, CONSERVATION AND CONTROL OF VITAL FORCE. By ELLA ADELIA FLETCHER, Author of "The Woman Beautiful," "The Philosophy of Rest." 372 pp., 4s. 6d. net.

"I regard it as the most important and authoritative contribution to 'Occult' science that has been made since Madame Blavatsky's publications, and it will reach and benefit multitudes who could never have profited by 'Isis Unveiled' or 'The Secret Doctrine'"

—JULIAN HAWTHORN.

"Written in clear English, and with moderation, as the result of both study and experiment the book is thoroughly 'up-to date'"—*T P S Book Notes*

PATHS TO POWER. By FLOYD B. WILSON, Author of "Man Limitless," "Through Silence to Realization," "The Discovery of the Soul" 229 pp, 4s 6d net.

"Thoughtfully written, and the truths the author wishes to teach, are presented in a very plain yet forcible manner"—*The Morning Advertiser*

THROUGH SILENCE TO REALIZATION; OR, THE HUMAN AWAKENING By FLOYD B. WILSON, Author of "Paths to Power," "Man Limitless," etc. 190pp., 3s. 6d net.

"This is an important, helpful and inspiring book, teaching man how to become all he is capable of being"—*Times Union*, Albany, N Y

"The chapter on 'The Silence' is the clearest practical exposition of the steps of human consciousness by which one reaches The Silence that we ever remember reading"—*Ideas*, Boston, Mass

THE DISCOVERY OF THE SOUL OUT OF MYSTI-CISM, LIGHT AND PROGRESS. By FLOYD B. WILSON, Author of "Paths to Power," "Man Limitless," etc 247 pp., 4s. 6d net.

An attempt is made herein to reveal the plane progressive man has attained on his ascent toward freedom, and to throw light on the path leading through Mysticism to the discovery of those unused powers within the soul which, duly appropriated, give expression to the divine in man

The following publications of Messrs. Fenno, of New York, are also supplied —:

MAN LIMITLESS. By FLOYD B. WILSON, Author of "Paths to Power." 224 pp, 4s. 6d. net.

"Have been reading your book, 'Man Limitless' It is brimful of energy, light, power and helpfulness from all sources"

—ELLA WHEELER WILCOX

THE TRIUMPH OF TRUTH; OR, THE DOOM OF DOGMA. By HENRY FRANK, Author of "The Kingdom of Love," "The Shrine of Silence," etc., etc., 6s. net.

"In this able work Mr. Frank has given a bold and radical treatise, which is at once broad and scholarly, and, what is still more rare in such works, reverent and constructive in spirit and character."
—*The Arena.*

"The 'Triumph of Truth' is an interesting work."—*The Athenæum.*

THE MASTERY OF MIND IN THE MAKING OF MAN. By HENRY FRANK, Author of "A Vision of the Invisible," "The Shrine of Silence," etc., etc. 234 pp., 4s. 6d. net.

"His arguments are based, not upon theory, but upon fact, and he sticks close to the indispensable data of physical science, and he has carefully studied his authorities"—*Annals of Psychical Science*

Alchemical Philosophy.

THE TAROT OF THE BOHEMIANS: The Most Ancient Book in the World, for the Exclusive Use of Initiates. By PAPUS. Translated from the French by A. P. MORTON. New edition, revised throughout, with introduction by A. E. WAITE. Crown 8vo, ornamental cloth gilt, gilt tops, 384pp., profusely illustrated, 6s. net.

"Probably the most complete exposition of the whole subject that can be obtained in the English language"—*Light.*

"Well illustrated, and garbed beautifully"—*The Theosophist.*

"M. Encausse's very considerable learning cannot be gainsaid."
—*Manchester Courier.*

A PACK OF 78 TAROT CARDS; Exquisitely drawn and coloured, from new and original designs by PAMELA COLEMAN SMITH. Each card has a separate allegorical meaning. This is without question the finest and most artistic pack that has ever been produced. Price 6s. net, in neat blue box, post free.

"The most wonderful pack of cards that has ever been seen since the days when Gringonneur illuminated three packs for the amusement of King Charles VI. of France, in the year of our Lord 1392."—Arthur Machen in *T. P.'s Weekly.*

the texts are concerned Crown 4to, gilt tops, 376pp., illustrated, with about 180 engravings, some of which are full page plates. Beautifully bound in Art Canvas, with Design in gold. Price 15s. net.

JUST PUBLISHED.

A MANUAL OF OCCULTISM. A complete Exposition of the Occult Arts and Sciences by SEPHARIAL, Author of "A Manual of Astrology," "Prognostic Astronomy," "Kabalistic Astrology," etc., etc. With numerous diagrams and illustrations. 368pp., handsomely bound in cloth gilt. Gilt tops. Crown 8vo., 6s. net.

CONTENTS

PART I.—THE OCCULT SCIENCES, comprising. Astrology—Palmistry—Thaumaturgy—Kabalism—Numerology—Talismans—Hypnotism.

PART II.—THE OCCULT ARTS, comprising Divination—The Tarot Cartomancy—Crystal Gazing—Clairvoyance—Geomancy—Psychometry—Dowsing—Dreams—Sortileges—Alchemy

The need for a concise and practical exposition of the main tenets of Occultism has long been felt In this manual of Occultism the author has dealt in a lucid manner with both the Occult Sciences and the Occult Arts, and has added some supplementary matter on the subjects of Hypnotism and Alchemy

The book is written from the point of view of a practical student, and contains many experimental results, which form valuable keys to the study and practice of the subjects dealt with. The text is, moreover, illustrated with numerous explanatory diagrams and symbols, and the whole work forms a more complete compendium of Occultism than any hitherto offered to the public, while it is supplied at a price well within the reach of the general reader

JUST PUBLISHED.

ALCHEMY: ANCIENT AND MODERN. Being a brief account of the Alchemistic Doctrines, and their relations, to mysticism on the one hand, and to recent discoveries in physical science on the other hand; together with some particulars regarding the lives and teachings of the most noted alchemists. By H. STANLEY REDGROVE, B.Sc. (Lond.), F.C.S., Author of "On the Calculation of Thermo-Chemical Constants,"

"Matter, Spirit and the Cosmos," etc With sixteen full-page illustrations (including Portraits of the most celebrated Alchemists). Demy 8vo , cloth gilt, 4s 6d. net.

CONTENTS —The Meaning of Alchemy—The Theory of Physical Alchemy—The Alchemists—The Outcome of Alchemy—The Age of Modern Chemistry—Modern Alchemy

YOUR FORTUNE IN YOUR NAME OR KABALISTIC ASTROLOGY New edition, largely revised. Demy 8vo, cloth gilt, 96 pp , 2s 6d net. By "SEPHARIAL."

The first edition of this popular work on Kabalistic Astrology having been entirely sold out, the publishers arranged with the author for this corrected and revised edition to meet the continued public demand

A MANUAL OF CARTOMANCY, Fortune Telling and Occult Divination, including the Oracle of Human Destiny, Cagliostro's Mystic Alphabet of the Magi, &c., &c. Fourth edition, greatly enlarged and revised, by GRAND ORIENT. Crown 8vo, cloth gilt, 252 pp., 2s. 6d. net.

"To the curious in such matters this book will afford much interesting information "—*Pall Mall Gazette*

NUMBERS, THEIR MAGIC AND MYSTERY. By Dr ISIDORE KOZMINSKY (Fra Ros. Crus.), F R.N.S., A.B A.A , Etc. Second Edition. Red paper covers, 6d. net.

An attempt to show how numbers can be used with prophetic accuracy in terrestrial affairs, with numerous examples

THE HERMETIC AND ALCHEMICAL WRITINGS OF AUREOLUS PHILIPPUS THEOPHRASTUS BOMBAST OF HOHENHEIM, CALLED PARACELSUS THE GREAT, now for the first time translated into English. Edited with a Biographical Preface, Elucidatory Notes, and a copious Hermetic Vocabulary and Index, by ARTHUR EDWARD WAITE. In Two Volumes. Dark Red Cloth. medium 4to, gilt tops. 25s. net. Vol. I., 394 pp. ; Vol II., 396 pp.

THE TURBA PHILOSOPHORUM, or Assembly of the Sages. An Ancient Alchemical Treatise, with the chief Readings of the Shorter Codex, Parallels from Greek Alchemists, and Explanations of obscure terms. Translated, with introduction and Notes, by A. E. WAITE. Crown 8vo., 4s. 6d. net.

A great symposium or debate of the Adepts assembled in convocation The work ranks next to Gober as a fountain-head of alchemy in Western Europe. It reflects the earliest Byzantine, Syrian and Arabian writers This famous work is accorded the highest place among the works of Alchemical Philosophy which are available for the students in the English language

THE NEW PEARL OF GREAT PRICE. The Treatise of Bonus concerning the Treasure of the Philosopher's Stone. Translated from the Latin. Edited by A. E. WAITE. Crown 8vo., 4s. 6s. net.

One of the classics of alchemy, with a very curious account, accompanied by emblematical figures, showing the generation and birth of metals, the death of those that are base and their resurrection in the perfect forms of gold and silver

A GOLDEN AND BLESSED CASKET OF NATURE'S MARVELS. BY BENEDICTUS FIGULUS. With a Life of the Author Edited by A. E. WAITE. Crown 8vo., 4s. 6d net.

A collection of short treatises by various authors belonging to the school of Paracelsus, dealing with the mystery of the Philosopher's Stone, the revelation of Hermes, the great work of the Tincture, the glorious antidote of Potable Gold Benedictus Figulus connects by imputation with the early Rosicrucians

THE TRIUMPHAL CHARIOT OF ANTIMONY By BASIL VALENTINE. Translated from the Latin, including the Commentary of Kerckringius, and Biographical and Critical Introduction. Edited by A. E. WAITE. Crown 8vo., 4s. 6d. net.

A valuable treatise by one who is reputed a great master of alchemical art. It connects practical chemistry with the occult theory of transmutation The antimonial Fire-Stone is said to cure diseases in man and to remove the imperfection of metals

THE ALCHEMICAL WRITINGS OF EDWARD KELLY. From the Latin Edition of 1676. With a Biographical Introduction, an Account of Kelly's relations with Dr. Dee, and a transcript of the "Book of St. Dunstan." Edited by A E. WAITE. Crown 8vo., 4s. 6d. net.

A methodised summary of the best Hermetic philosophers, including a discourse on Terrestrial Astronomy, in which the planets are replaced by metals, and instead of an account of stellar influences we have the laws governing metallic conversion

Mental Pathology and Therapeutics

THE MASTERY OF DEATH. By A. OSBORNE EAVES Author of "The Colour Cure" Crown 8vo Cloth, 2s. net.

The object of this work is to show how disease may be eliminated and human life almost indefinitely prolonged, and the writer gives clear directions as to how these aims can be accomplished

THE ART OF LUCK. By A. OSBORNE EAVES. Author of "The Colour Cure," "The Mastery of Death," etc. 5in. × $4\frac{3}{4}$in, paper covers, 1s net.

"It is better to be born lucky than rich"—OLD PROVERB

SYNOPSIS —Life's Failures Human Fossils The True Source of Luck Forces and Planes The Dynamics of Thought Socrates' Demon How Magic can Aid Lucky days and Astrology The Science of Numbers Talismans and Charms as Auxiliaries Mind Control and Building Recipe for Weak Wills, etc

IMAGINATION THE MAGICIAN. By A OSBORNE EAVES, author of "The Colour Cure," etc. Paper covers, 1s. net.

THE COLOUR CURE. A Popular Exposition of the Use of Colour in the Treatment of Disease, by A. OSBORNE EAVES, Author of "The Mastery of Death," etc., etc. Crown 8vo, 64 pp., paper covers, 1s. 6d. net.

ELEMENTARY TEXT-BOOK OF MENTAL THERAPEUTICS. By W. J. COLVILLE. Crown 8vo, paper covers, 80 pp., 1s. net.

This introductory text book is characterised by all Mr W J Colville's well known simplicity and perspicuity of style. For practical guidance in every-day life it is of far greater value than many more expensive and more ambitious volumes

PSYCHO-PATHOLOGICAL RESEARCHES. Studies in Mental Dissociation. With Text Figures and 10 Plates. By BORIS SIDIS, M.A., Ph.D., Director of the Psycho-pathological Laboratory of New York. 329 pp., Royal 8vo, 8s. 6d. net.

SELECTION FROM THE CONTENTS —Psychosis and Introspection The Subjective Method and its Difficulties. Examination of the Subconscious. The Psychopathic Paradox Subconscious Habit Formation. Automatic Writing and Anaesthesia. Origin and Growth of Dissociation. The Development of the Secondary State. The Synthesis of the Dissociated States. The Phenomena of Affective Triple Personality Re-emergence of Disintegrated Groups and their Final Dissolution Dissociation and Synthesis. First Attacks and Aura Lapsed Periods and Hypnoidal States Synthesis.

READY MARCH 1st.

ABNORMAL PSYCHOLOGY. By ISADOR H. CORIAT, M.D., Second Assistant Physician for Diseases of the Nervous System, Boston City Hospital, Neurologist to the Mt. Sinai Hospital. Crown 8vo, cloth gilt, 322 pp., 5s. net.

CONTENTS.

I. THE EXPLORATION OF THE SUBCONSCIOUS.—What is the Subconscious?—Automatic Writing—Testing the Emotions—Analysing the Emotions—Sleep—Dreams—What is Hypnosis?—Analysis of the Mental Life

II DISEASES OF THE SUBCONSCIOUS —Losses of Memory—Restoration of Lost Memories—Illusions of Memory—The Splitting of a Personality — Hysteria — Psychasthenia — Neurasthenia — Psycho-Epileptic Attacks.

Most of the investigations on Abnormal Psychology are widely scattered throughout the pages of medical publications and psychological literature generally Hence these researches are difficult of access to the general reader in any convenient and connected form.

The present volume is an attempt to bring all this material together within the compass of a single work, and some personal observations and experiments have been supplied by the Author in illustration of the various theories propounded The book is a valuable study of psychological phenomena in the region of the abnormal, and especially of subconscious mental states, from the medical standpoint

Ars Vivendi Publications.

ARS VIVENDI or The Art of Living and acquiring Mental and Bodily Vigour. By ARTHUR LOVELL. 2s. net.

" A sensible treatise of encouraging advice and instruction."
—*Scotsman*

CONCENTRATION. By ARTHUR LOVELL. 2s. net.

" Concentration is the supremest art, and we are grateful for the author's insistence upon it."—*Pall Mall Gazette.*

VOLO or THE WILL. What it is, How to Strengthen and How to use it. By ARTHUR LOVELL. 2s. 6d. net.

" It is a clearly written book, designed to tell people how to strengthen and how to use the will."—*Scotsman*

IMAGINATION and its Wonders. By ARTHUR LOVELL. 5s. net.

" Mr Lovell first of all considers his great subject from the scientific view point, and concludes a valuable book by two admirably written chapters 'Verifying the Imagination' and 'Right Use of Imagination.' "—*The Idler.*

BEAUTY OF TONE IN SPEECH AND SONG. By ARTHUR LOVELL 1s. net.

" Mr. Lovell has here a discovery which will raise the standard of voice cultivation to a high level "—*Times.*

DEEP BREATHING. By ARTHUR LOVELL. 1s net.

" Discusses an important subject in all its bearings, and incisively and luminously expounds some very sagacious counsels "
—*Leicester Post.*

HOW TO THINK. By ARTHR LOVELL. 1s. net.

" A grammar of mental language."—*Scotsman.*

164 Aldersgate Street, London, E.C.

Rider's Mind and Body Handbooks.

These Handbooks deal with the subject of mental and bodily health in the new light of psycho-therapeutics, mental healing and auto-suggestion. The following volumes are now ready or in preparation:—

NATURE'S HELP TO HAPPINESS. By JOHN WARREN ACHORN, M.D. Small crown 8vo., 55 pp., cloth gilt, 1/- net, paper, 6d. net.

"A suggestive essay on the benefits of the open-air life."—*The Scotsman.*

"This is the best book ever written on health"—*Equinox.*

HOW TO REST AND BE RESTED. By GRACE DAWSON. 46 pp. red paper cover, 6d. net, cloth, 1s. net.

It is the purpose of this little book to point out practically the restful way of living . . . Wrong to the body is wrong to the mind and to the spirit. The whole man—body, soul and spirit—must live in unity and harmony in order to realise a full and healthy life

"This little book is especially to be recommended to those who dread the possibility of a nerve breakdown"—*Nursing Notes.*

"Brief and to the point, it contains in 46 pages as much common sense as many a bulky volume"—*Health Record.*

NERVOUSNESS: A Brief and Popular Review of the Moral Treatment of Disordered Nerves. By ALFRED T. SCHOFIELD, M.D., M.R.C.S. Small crown 8vo., cloth gilt, 88pp., 1s. net.

"A medical manifesto of real importance . . . It is not too much to say that if Dr. Schofield's principles were acted upon, they would lead to something like a revolution in the treatment of nervous sufferers . . . a singularly wise and able little book."
—*Westminster Gazette.*

"Wise counsels for the prevention of nervous disorders."
—*Christian World.*

"Dr. Schofield states his case well . . . the book is well worth reading."—*The Queen.*

THE POWER OF SELF-SUGGESTION. By Rev. SAMUEL McCOMB, D D Small crown 8vo , cloth gilt, 1,- net.

"A readable and stimulating essay "—*Scotsman*

" A well-written essay, free from technicality on the one hand and from emotional exaggeration on the other "—*T P S Book Notes*

HOW TO KEEP FIT. An Unconventional Manual. By ALFRED SCHOFIELD, M.D., M.R.C.S. Author of "Nervousness," etc., etc Small crown 8vo., cloth gilt, 80 pp , 1s. net.

A wise little Book "—*The Observer.*

"Full of really sound and sensible advice "—*Newcastle Daily Chronicle*

" It ought to prove extremely helpful to all those who desire to live rationally "—*Yorkshire Evening Post*

" A useful little manual on personal hygiene "—*Scotsman*

" Hints on health which are given in a rational, common-sense way, which is refreshingly unusual in works of the kind "—*Irish Times*

" A suggestive health manual, which has the rare virtue of not encouraging the faddist or the valetudinarian in their ways "
—*Birmingham Daily Post.*

" This book is well worth reading "—*Christian World*

FROM PASSION TO PEACE; or, THE PATHWAY OF THE PURE. By JAMES ALLEN. Author of "The Mastery of Destiny," " From Poverty to Power," "As a Man Thinketh," etc., etc. Small crown 8vo., cloth gilt, 72 pp., 1s net

The first three parts of this book--*Passion*, *Aspiration* and *Temptation*—represent the common human life, with its passion, pathos and tragedy , the last three parts—*Transcendence*, *Beatitude* and *Peace*—present the Divine Life, calm, wise and beautiful, of the sage and Saviour The middle part--*Transmutation*—is the transitional stage between the two , it is the alchemic process linking the divine with the human life Discipline, denial and renunciation do not constitute the Divine State, they are only the means by which it is attained The Divine Life is established in that Perfect Knowledge which bestows Perfect Peace

"This thoughtful little book"—*Publishers' Circular*

"A delightful little book with a strong Buddhistic tendency"
—*Annals of Psychical Science*

NOW READY.

STUDIES IN SELF-HEALING, or Cure by Meditation. A practical application of the principles of the true mystic healing of the ages. By ERNEST E. MUNDAY. Small crown 8vo., 79 pp. Cloth gilt. 1s. net.

"Full of interesting and useful materials . . offers many practical suggestions"—*Two Worlds*

THE INFLUENCE OF THE MIND ON THE BODY. By Dr. PAUL DUBOIS, Professor of Neuro-Pathology in the University of Berne, Author of "The Psychic Treatment of Nervous Disorders," "Self-Control, and How to Secure It," etc. Translated from the Fifth French Edition by L. B. GALLATIN. Small crown 8vo, 64 pp., cloth gilt, 1s net.

"A clearly-stated study of an extremely interesting subject"
—*Scotsman*

"Will afford the student much food for thought, whilst it is simple enough to appeal even to those who are comparatively ignorant of this subject"—*Sunday Times.*

"A very wise book."—*Light,*

"An excellent work containing most sound advice for those who make their own life and the lives of their families a misery through the worry habit"—*Manchester Courier*

Theology.

THE UNESCAPEABLE CHRIST. And Other Sermons An expression of the New Theology. By Rev. EDWARD W. LEWIS, M A, B.D, of Grafton Square Congregational Church, Clapham Author of "Some Views of Modern Theology." Crown 8vo, cloth, 3s 6d net.

"The author frankly declares himself a disciple of the New Theology, and the sermons are all upon subjects which are involved in that controversy They are marked by great freshness and beauty, and will do much to remove prejudice against the new views"—*Scotsman*

SOME BETTER THING FOR US. By A. S. L. Second Impression. Demy 12mo, cloth gilt, 3s. 6d. net

CONTENTS—Introduction Faith A Practical Matter Fear Its true Function Truth in Relation to Life Error in Thought, and its Dangers The Law of the Lord The Law which Gendereth Bondage The Two Points of View The Threefold Cord of Prayer Object Lessons of Christ's Methods in Healing Health, Holiness and Power

This volume is addressed specially to that large class of sufferers, whose trials have not found adequate support in the presentment of religion which has come their way

"A lucid exposition of the efficacy of faith"—*Light*

"The expression of a living faith, which has been tested by experience."—H A DALLAS in *The Seeker*

GOD THE BEAUTIFUL, An Artist's Creed; and The Religion of Beauty Contrasted with Buddhism. By E P.B. Second Edition (translated into Japanese and German). Fcap. 8vo., 2s. 6d. net.

"The writer's philosophy may be described as a kind of pantheistic idealism He finds a manifestation of 'God the Beautiful' in Nature, in the soul of man, in all acts of human love and courage . . The book contains many suggestive, original and beautiful thoughts" —*Church Quarterly Review*

TRANSFORMED HINDUISM. By the Author of "God the Beautiful." 2 Vols. Fcap 8vo, 5s. net.

CONTENTS.—Vol. I.—Introduction. Panorama of Ancient India. Development of India's Commerce. The Rise of Brahmanism. The Spiritual Empire of India. The Sacred Scriptures: Rig Veda, Soma Veda, Yajur Veda, Atharva Veda. The Brahmanas, Aranyaki and Upanishads. The Fivefold Ministry. The Legal Works, Dharma Sutras, &c.

CONTENTS.—Vol. II.—Hindu Philosophical Systems. The Nyaya and Vaiseshika, The Sankhya, The Yoga, The Purva Mimansa, The Vedanta School. Epics: The Mahabharata, The Bhagavat Gita, The Ramayana, Modern Hinduism. Sin. Death and Immortality.

"It is well written, and gives a comprehensive view of Brahmanism, of 'the sacred scriptures,' Hindu philosophical systems, and the Hindu epics, modern Hinduism, etc."—*The Times.*

THE CHIEF SCRIPTURE OF INDIA. (*The Bhagavad Gita*) and its relation to present events. By W. L. WILMSHURST, Author of "Christianity and Science: The Latest Phase," &c. Crown 8vo. Cloth, 2s. net.

"An introduction to the study of the *Bhagavad Gita*, calling attention to its relation to the Western religious thought of the present day. A thoughtful and well written paper by a widely read man, who hopes that some day, in the inevitable course of the world's evolution, all races of men will form 'one fold under one shepherd.'"—*Academy*.

"A brief and interesting general account of the *Bhagavad Gita*, which may well serve as an introduction to the detailed study of that Sacred Book of the East."—*Scotsman*

CHILDREN OF THE RESURRECTION. By THOS. ALLEN. Crown 8vo. Paper cover, 6d. net.

CONTENTS.—Introduction. Eschatology. The Recession of the Soul. Spiritual Corporeity. The Power of Christ's Resurrection. The Nature of Christ's Resurrection. Eclectic Resurrection. Equality in Heaven (*a*) Dead-levelism (*b*) Disciplinary Treatment (*c*) Formation of Character. Eternal Life.

THE MESSAGE OF ARCHDEACON WILBERFORCE. A Summary of the Teaching found in his Sermons and Discourses. By a member of the Congregation of St. John's, Westminster. Crown 8vo. Paper cover, 6d. net.

THE MESSAGE OF THE SUN, AND THE CULT OF THE CROSS AND THE SERPENT. By Rev HOLDEN E SAMPSON ("Light.") Crown 8vo., 1s. 6d. net

"The cult here advocated, under the fantastic title of the 'Cult of the Cross and the Serpent,' was, according to Mr Sampson, taught in its purity by Moses and the Hebrew Prophets, by Krishna and Christ, but was effaced from the world through the heresies of the *Nicene Apostasy* until now re-discovered by himself at the end of fourteen centuries. Judaism and Christianity are perversions of this true and only religion"—*Sheffield Daily Telegraph*

CHRISTIANITY AND SCIENCE—THE LATEST PHASE. By W L WILMSHURST. Crown 8vo., 92 pp., in neat brown paper cover 6d. net, cloth 1s. net.

CONTENTS—Foreword The Parting of the Ways The Development of the Conflict New Factors tending to Reconciliation The Present and the Future

"The treatment of the subject is thorough"—*Light*

LIVING THE LIFE; or, CHRISTIANITY IN BEING. By GRACE DAWSON. Author of "How to Rest and be Rested. Crown 8vo., 78 pp., cloth gilt, gilt tops, 1s. 6d. net; paper, 1s. net.

A short study of Christianity as Christ taught it.

"Devout and intelligent religious discourses"—*Scotsman.*

NOW READY.

THE FIRST CHRISTIAN GENERATION. Its Records and Traditions. Second and cheaper Edition. By JAMES THOMAS, Author of "Our Records of the Nativity,' "The Pantheon at Rome: Who Built It?" 414 pp. Red cloth, gilt. Crown 8vo., 3s. 6d. net.

SELECTION FROM CONTENTS—The Interment, Resurrection and Ascension—Narrative of Acts—Paul's Earlier Life—Paul's Later Journeys—Authorship and Reliability of the Acts—Peter and Paul at Rome—The Remaining Gospel Characters—The Church in Jerusalem—Exterior Churches

The author of this book aims at presenting a truthful account of the earliest Christian times, in so far as this can be reconstructed from such records and documents as survive Among these, the latter part of the composite document, Luke-Acts (the former part having been dealt with in a previous work), has been carefully examined, and an attempt is made to arrive at a final appreciation, from an independent point of view, of the position of the creed and organisation of the primitive Christian churches, having regard to their relationship with the political and social movements of the period. The writer's chief object is to discriminate myth from fact in the incidents narrated, and the debatable territory of doctrine has been avoided as far as possible.

The unbiassed reader will find the author's sane and scholarly criticism and sound judgment in agreeable contrast to what is generally submitted in the guise of an historical estimate of this much-discussed epoch to an over-indulgent public

READY FEBRUARY 1st.

THE NEW GOD AND OTHER ESSAYS. By RALPH SHIRLEY, Editor of "The Occult Review" Crown 8vo, cloth gilt, 3s. 6d net.

Poetry.

STRANGE HOUSES OF SLEEP. By ARTHUR EDWARD WAITE. With Frontispiece Portrait of the Author. F'cap. 4to. Parchment gilt Printed at the Ballantyne Press. 12s. net. Limited Edition of 250 copies, signed and numbered.

Part I Shadows of Sacraments Part II The Hidden Sacrament of The Holy Graal Part III The Poor Brother's Mass Book containing a Method of Assisting at the Holy Sacrifice for children who are not of this world There is also implied a certain assistance to Servers Part IV The Book of the King's Dole, and Chantry for Plain Song A Greater Initiation

"Sciendum est igitur, dona omnia, in quibus vita nostra consistit, sacramentis et externis quibusdam sensibilibus signis tecta ac involuta esse"

"Through all one comes in touch with a fine spirit, alive to the glory of the world and all that charms the heart and sense of man, yet seeing past these with something of the soul of Galahad Rich in memorable verse and significant thought, so closely wedded to emotion that each seems either"—*Glasgow Herald*

A BOOK OF MYSTERY AND VISION. By ARTHUR EDWARD WAITE. Foolscap 4to, with Special Cover designed by MARY TOURTEL, and Frontispiece by ISABELLE DE STEIGER. Price 7s. 6d. net.

"The most remarkable and on the whole the most successful attempt to sing the mysteries of mysticism, since Blake wrote his 'Prophetic Books.'"—*The Star*

"There is true gold of poetry in the book, and often more of real thought and suggestiveness in a single page than would go to the making of a whole volume of average minor verse."—*The Bookman.*

"Undoubtedly one of the most original and most remarkable books of verse published for many years"—*Birmingham Daily Gazette*

"Mr Waite's volume may be regarded as a confession and an exposition of faith of the mystic school"—*Glasgow Herald*

JUST PUBLISHED.

THE BRAHMAN'S WISDOM. Translated from the German of Friedrich Ruckert. By EVA M. MARTIN. Small crown 8vo. Bound with artistic design in violet and lemon cloth, gilt. 1s. 6d. net.

Friedrich Rückert was born at Schweinfurt in 1788 During a long life he published many volumes of poetry, of which perhaps one of the best known is the *Weisheit des Brahmanen*, published in 1836. It treats of all imaginable subjects, from the deepest problems of existence, and the beauties of Nature and Art, down to the smallest details of human daily life. The book, as a whole, breathes a sane and lofty philosophy of life, and teems with thoughts and phrases of a rare and original charm Nearly all the stanzas in the collection have been taken from the first two sections of the book Ruckert has well been named in Germany a "Master of Form." His resources of both rhyme and metre—and of the former in particular—are apparently endless. He wields the rich and sonorous German words with something of the same consummate ease which Swinburne showed in moulding our English language into new forms of melody and rhythm.

THE NAZARENE: The Study of a Man. A Poem. By ARTHUR H. ADAMS, Author of "Maoriland and other Verses." Demy 8vo, cloth gilt, 2s. 6d. net.

"His work is reverent and sincere, and not without dramatic force."—*Times.*

Belles Lettres.

The Aldwych Series

Edited by ALFRED H HYATT

Printed in red and black on hand-made paper at the Cedar Press, and bound in vellum. End-papers designed by DUDLEY HEATH. 3s. 6d. net per vol.

Not more than 300 copies printed of any single volume.

I. **CUPID'S POSIES.** Mottoes for Rings and other Pleasant Things.

II. **A LITTLE BOOK OF GRACES.**

"This little anthology should have a wide appeal "—*T.P's Weekly.*

"One of the prettiest compilations of the year . an altogether charming little volume "—*Glasgow Herald*

III. **A GARDEN OF SPIRITUAL FLOWERS.** An Elizabethan Book of Devotions: containing prayers for each day of the week, and others for sundry occasions.

" The true simplicity, joyous, strong and grand, is to be found in these prayers "—T H L. in *The Occult Review*

IV. **ROSE-LEAVES FROM SADI'S GARDEN.** Being the "Gulistan" rendered into Verse by ALFRED H. HYATT.

"From the 'Gulistan,' or Rose Garden of Sadi, these leaves have been gathered Sadi, whose name signifies felicity, was born at Shiraz in Persia, A D 1194 It is said that he lived a hundred and two years The whole of his long life was devoted to the accumulation of knowledge gained during his many travels Some of Sadi's wise thoughts are here set forth "—*From the Foreword* —A H H

"The reflective wisdom of Sadi has been gracefully interpreted by Mr Alfred H Hyatt "—*Nottingham Daily Guardian*

(Only a few copies of the first three volumes of THE ALDWYCH BOOKLETS remain for sale)

THE PAGEANT OF SUMMER. By RICHARD JEFFERIES. *Edition de Luxe* of 100 copies Printed at the Chiswick Press on Van Gelder Paper. Decorated by DUDLEY HEATH. White vellum. F'cap. 4to. 7s. 6d. net

This Edition is printed by arrangement with Messrs Chatto & Windus, the owners of the Copyright

A very charming miniature example of artistic book-production In its chaste vellum binding, with its decorative lettering and its perfection of paper and type, the little volume presents Jefferies' exquisite prose poem in a form worthy of its rare intrinsic beauty as a work of literary art "—*The World*

LORD CHESTERFIELD'S ADVICE TO HIS SON AND THE POLITE PHILOSOPHER. Crown 8vo., cloth, gilt, 1s. 6d. net.

' A plain, tastefully produced volume, in clear type on light paper, well and attractively arranged Lord Chesterfield can always be ' witty without satire, and serious without being dull ', and in spite of its age his wisdom is fresh to-day, and no unsafe guide in this form for any young man beginning his career "—*The Bookman*

Fiction.

THE THRONE OF EDEN: A Psychical Romance. By W. J. COLVILLE, Author of "Old and New Psychology," "Studies in Theosophy," etc., etc. Crown 8vo., red cloth, 468 pp , 3s. 6d net

" Much profound philosophy is intermingled with amusing incidents of various kinds "—*Fischer-Munck Leigh*

THE DAYS OF FIRE. The Story of a Forgotten Epoch. By the COUNTESS OF CROMARTIE. Crown 8vo., 2s.6d. net,

An idyll of love and strife in the days of Heremon, King of Erin, who reigned in Tara

" The story of a forgotten epoch, told with skill and feeling "
—*Times*

" Written with a fine romantic fancy, and with many happy turns of invention, it cannot fail to please anyone interested in the legendary heroes of Erin "—*Scotsman*

HIS PRIVATE LIFE. By H. SMITH. New Edition Crown 8vo, 3s. 6d net.

"The story is developed with a strong and practised hand many well-drawn personalities'—*Morning Post*

"A novel that has much truth in it, treated with striking ability"—*The Evening Standard and St James's Gazette*

"The minor characters are exceedingly well drawn, and the novel stands out from the great ruck of fiction, both by its maturity of touch and power of construction"—*T P's Weekly*

"A novel of exceptional ability'—*Review of Reviews*

THE PRIESTESS OF ISIS. An Occult Romance of the Days of Pompeii, by ÉDOUARD SCHURE. Translated by F ROTHWELL, B A Crown 8vo, 318 pp., cloth gilt, 3s. 6d. net.

"It pictures with much graphic power the City of Pompeii on the eve of her destruction"—*The Times*

"Powerfully written and well conceived, this novel is sure to interest a great number of readers"—*Daily Telegraph*

"A classical drama full of colour and poetry"—*Yorkshire Post*

THE SECRET OF THE SPHINX; or, The Ring of Moses. By JAMES SMITH and JOHN WREN SUTTON. Crown 8vo, 3s. 6d. net.

"A romance, founded on the building of the Great Pyramid by Pharaoh and the birth of Moses, is a distinctly notable addition to modern fiction, and Mr Smith and Mr Sutton have done their work conscientiously and well The secret of the Sphinx is revealed by a narrative of a curious combination of circumstances, in which the magic ring of Moses is given a conspicuous place"—*The Scotsman*

"A vividly drawn and fascinating picture of life in Egypt and the desert, and interprets on broad and universal principles the 'wisdom of the Egyptians' in which Moses was learned"—*Light*

GRAN; A Girl Worth Knowing. By H. D'ARCY MARTIN. Crown 8vo, 3s. 6d. net.

"The upbringing of Gran amidst surroundings so unusual—a stern, fanatical father, a reserved mother who nurses a secret and cares nothing for her child, leaving her to the sole charge of an old servant—and the development of her character, are portrayed with considerable power, the result being a very charming picture"—*Literary World*

"Gran is remarkable, and also a remarkably attractive heroine"—*Sheffield Telegraph.*

"There is not a dull sentence in the book"—*Review of Reviews*

THE LIVING WHEEL. By T. I. UNIACKE. A Drama in Five Acts. Crown 8vo, 3s. 6d. net.

This story of a spiritual marriage presents strange possibilities of union between those who are of necessity separated in the physical body.

"This is one of the most remarkable books that I have read for many a long day. A daring book, a puzzling book, one that suggests more than it says, and raises questions innumerable to which it supplies no answers."—W T STEAD, in *The Review of Reviews.*

"A thoughtfully written novel, and one that dips a little deeper than most into spiritual and intellectual matters"—*T P's Weekly.*

THE TWICE-BORN. By an Ex-Associate of the Society for Psychical Research. Crown 8vo, cloth, 2s. net.

A modern instance of Re-incarnation as exemplified in the case of two children—brother and sister—who revisit the earth after a very short interval, so that they are enabled to retain a vivid impression of their previous state of existence

"A fascinating tale. . . The author is evidently a person of great originality of thought, and also well versed in psychic mysteries."

—*Progressive Thought.*

THE SOUND OF A VOICE THAT IS STILL. By ARCHIE CAMPBELL. Cheaper Issue. Crown 8vo, 3s. 6d. net.

"Can certainly claim to be the most original work of the year. A combination of romance and theology, or perhaps we should say mythology, it provides, in the form of a story, a new theory of life, death, and eternity, derived from Eastern teaching, Christian doctrine, and romantic imagination, which is as fascinating as it is delightful.

An interesting and a fascinating book which merits the attention it has already aroused."—*Birmingham Daily Gazette*

FLAXIUS: Leaves from the Life of an Immortal. By CHARLES GODFREY LELAND, Author of "The Breitmann Ballads," &c. Crown 8vo, 3s. 6d. net.

"Mr Godfrey Leland, apart from the keen sense of humour which inspired the 'Hans Breitmann Ballads,' has a great deal of old-world knowledge at his command. Both the humour and the knowledge jostle one another in 'Flaxius,' a book which is rather a rhapsody than a romance. Flaxius is an Immortal, and into his lips Mr Leland puts his own philosophy of Life. There are passages in the book which are an invitation to think, and they stand side by side with much elaborate fooling."—*Standard.*

"It is quite impossible to give any idea of this book. It is enough, surely, to say that it is Mr Leland's to send people of sense to it. But we may thank him for many excellent things in it, and not the least for the Breitmann ballad with which it is concluded"—*Spectator*

THE LIFE AND CONFESSION OF ASENATH, the Daughter of Pentephres of Heliopolis. Narrating how the All-Beautiful Joseph took her to Wife. Prepared by MARY BRODRICK, from notes supplied by the late SIR PETER LE PAGE RENOUF. Crown 8vo. paper covers, 1s. net. Exquisitely printed on hand-made paper.

The Life and Confession of Asenath, the Daughter of Pentephres of Heliopolis, is one of those many quaint little stories of a religious character which appear to have had their rise somewhere about the 6th century A.D. It is undoubtedly written with a purpose—to reconcile early Christian converts to the idea of Joseph (a type of Christ) taking unto himself the daughter of the high priest of false gods and herself an idolater. The little story recounts the preparations made for the reception of Joseph who was making a tour in Egypt to prepare for the coming famine, Asenath's arrogance towards "the runaway" and slave, her final conversion to his religion when she "flung her gods out of the window," and her marriage to Joseph. The story has much spirit and life in it; it is a strange medley of Egyptian, Jewish and Christian religious ideas, but it has a charm and poetry about it which cannot fail to interest the lovers of ancient lore.

The Library of Occult Records.

Crown 8vo, in artistically designed blue cloth, gilt lettering. 3s. 6d. net per volume.

This Library is designed to include a selection from the best Occult and Psychic stories which lay claim to an inspirational origin. No fiction of the ordinary stamp will be given a place among these books. The following volumes are now ready:—

THROUGH THE MISTS. Leaves from the Autobiography of a Soul in Paradise. Recorded for the Author by ROBERT JAMES LEES. 3s. 6d. net.

"An extremely fascinating story."—*Yorkshire Post*

"Mr Lees acts merely as recorder, and his work should have much of the vogue that fell to 'Letters from Hell' on the one hand, and 'Letters from Julia' on the other"—*Academy.*

"Mr Lees' story is supremely fascinating"—*Birmingham Gazette*

"It is reverent, poetical and quite ingenious in conception It will appeal especially to Spiritualists, many of whose religious beliefs it embodies."—*Manchester Courier.*

THE LIFE ELYSIAN. Being More Leaves from the Autobiography of a Soul in Paradise. Recorded for the Author by R. J. LEES. 349 pp., 3s. 6d. net.

"Whoever takes up this book will be loth to lay it down till the last page is reached."—*Liverpool Courier.*

"A very curious and interesting book"—*The Lady*

"It is an impressive work, of a most unusual type, and even those readers who take exception to the doctrines set forth will be repaid for their trouble by much that is suggestive and inspiring"—*Court Circular*

THE CAR OF PHŒBUS. By R. J. LEES. 388 pp., 3s. 6d. net.

"A well-told story of love, adventure and political intrigue in the days when the great powers of Babylon and Egypt were yet rising towards the zenith of their glory. . . . Decidedly interesting."—*To-Day*

"Thoroughly readable."—*Punch*

"A clever mystical romance."—*Light.*

"A passionate love story . . . It is very powerfully written, and takes, what is so rare to find, a new and uncommon line."—*Queen.*

THE HERETIC. By Robert James Lees. 566 pp., 3s 6d. net.

"Decidedly curious and interesting."—*Morning Leader*

"A very original story."—*Lloyd's Weekly*

"The book is an able production, and is an honest attempt at solving the problem of human existence."—*Dundee Advertiser.*

"In 'The Heretic' Mr Lees has produced a thoughtful work that will certainly appeal to a very wide circle."—*Catholic Herald.*

AN ASTRAL BRIDEGROOM: A Reincarnation Study. By Robert James Lees. 404 pp., 3s. 6d. net.

"Mr Lees has . . . succeeded in producing a most interesting story, in which both tragedy and comedy are admirably blended, while occult experiences occur on almost every page."

—*Annals of Psychical Science*

"Not only a clever and original, but in some parts a humorous novel."—*The Christmas Bookseller*

IDA LLYMOND AND HER HOUR OF VISION. By Hope Cranford. 3s. 6d. net.

"This story will please and edify many readers; it is a novel and reverent treatise on a thorny problem."—*The English Review*

"Its machinery is elaborate yet simple. . . . Always a burning faith in the all-wisdom of the Father of all . . . It expresses many uplifting thoughts in graceful language, and is the sort of book that makes a deep impression on the responsive mind."—*Aberdeen Free Press*

"There is more than a tendency to mysticism in the contents of this volume. Its tone is distinctly religious. . Ida Llymond is brought low by illness, and her mind, bordering on the infinite, has an open vision of the life beyond the veil. She thinks she obtains an insight into the hidden meaning of many things, and a knowledge of the beatific condition of those who have entered into rest"—*Birmingham Post*

"The tone and moral teaching are of the highest The book should find a large circle of readers"—*Sheffield Telegraph.*

Controversial.

INFERENCES FROM HAUNTED HOUSES AND HAUNTED MEN. By Hon. JOHN HARRIS. Crown 8vo, 1s. net.

'There is a great deal in the volume which will interest those who love to explore the 'occult' branches of science"—*Westminster Review.*

"We recommend it to all interested in the subject"—*Spectator.*

"Curious readers of curious subjects may find it worth while to look into what Mr Harris says"—*New York Times*

THE PSEUDO-OCCULT. Notes on Telepathic Vision and Auditory Messages proceeding from Hypnotism. By Hon. JOHN HARRIS. Crown 8vo, 1s. net.

"Students of psychical research will find much to interest them"
—*Aberdeen Free Press.*

THE ALTERNATE SEX, or The Female Intellect in Man and the Masculine in Woman. By CHARLES GODFREY LELAND, F.R.L.S., A.M., Harvard. New and Cheaper Edition. Crown 8vo, cloth, 2s. 6d. net.

CONTENTS.—Absolute Difference of Sex The Origin of Life, or how it is that "Things" grow. The Origin of Sex. The Female Mind in Man, its Influence on the Inner Self—Occultism and Spiritualism. The Male Intellect in Woman. Dreams. Memory Hypnotism. Sensitivity and Love. On Entering into Harmony and Sympathy with the Inner Mind Of Mutual Influence. The Immortality of the Soul The Existence of God

"A curious theory of the psychology of sex . . The chief point of the theory is that every man has so much woman in his nature every woman so much man in hers"—*Scotsman*

"The book is the fruit of wide eclectic reading, and is in line with the best thought of the time"—*Daily News*.

TEKEL; or, The Wonderland of the Bible. By J. Horton. A Sequel to "My Search for Truth and What I Found." Demy 8vo, cloth gilt, 6s. net.

"In many respects a clever, fascinating, and wholesome piece of writing, and in all respects an honest and sincere work"—

Glasgow Evening Times

The Shilling Library of Psychical Literature and Inquiry.

Demy 8vo. Vols. I. II. III. IV. 1s. net each, paper covers; 1s. 6d. net, neatly bound in green cloth.

By Edward T. Bennett

Assistant Secretary to the Society for Psychical Research, 1882–1902.

I. THE SOCIETY FOR PSYCHICAL RESEARCH: Its Rise and Progress, and a Sketch of its Work.

Principal Contents.—The Society for Psychical Research Its Rise and Progress Thought-Transference or Telepathy. Suggestion—Hypnotism—Psychic Healing The Subliminal Self. Apparitions and Hauntings. Evidence of the Existence of Intelligences other than "The Living," and of the Reality of Inter-communication. Conclusions.

II. TWENTY YEARS OF PSYCHICAL RESEARCH: 1882-1901

Principal Contents. — Twenty Years of Psychical Research: 1882-1901. The Work Accomplished Its Character and Amount. Evidence of the Phenomena, Arranged under Three Groups. Conclusions. A Descriptive Index of References to Main Issues

·I. and II. are Illustrated with Facsimiles of Thought-Transference Drawings.

III. AUTOMATIC SPEAKING AND WRITING: A STUDY With many hitherto Unpublished Cases and Examples

PRINCIPAL CONTENTS —I Automatic Speaking and Writing II Communications which state definite Facts, or in which Information is conveyed unknown by any normal means to Speaker or Writer Some Incidents in a Business Transaction III Communications in which the Intelligence claims to give Evidence of its Identity with a Deceased Person Messages from Twenty-one alleged "Strangers," with more or less complete Verifications, A Test arranged before Death Professor J H Hyslop's Investigation and Testimony IV Communications the chief interest of which lies in their character Selections from the Records of a Private Circle V The Sources of the Communications, and Conclusions A Descriptive Catalogue of (English) Automatic Literature

IV. THE "DIRECT" PHENOMENA OF SPIRITUALISM.—"DIRECT" WRITING, DRAWING, PAINTING, and MUSIC.

This book is a Study of "Direct" Phenomena, mostly in the presence of David Duguid and of Mrs Everitt. Great care has been taken as to the quality of the evidence selected The volume is extensively illustrated with a unique series of Facsimiles of "Direct" Writings and Drawings Also with reproductions of certain engravings alleged to have been plagiarised As to these, a hitherto unrecognised form of Telepathy is suggested as the solution of the singular resemblances Twenty-two plates in all

"Spiritualists will read the book with interest, and the curious inquirer will derive both enlightenment and entertainment from its pages"—*Scotsman*

GLOBES AND MIRRORS FOR CRYSTAL GAZING.

Small size globe, 2s. 3d. post free in United Kingdom (including case), abroad 2s 9d

Z-rays globe (superior quality), 3s 3d post free in United Kingdom (including case), abroad 3s 9d

Larger globe (2½in diameter), 4s 9d post free in United Kingdom, abroad 5s. 3d

Small Fakir Mirror, 3s 6d net, Post Free, in United Kingdom, abroad, 4s, post free